TIPS AND TRICKS
FOR TRADING STOCKS
IN THE NIGERIAN STOCK MARKET &
MANAGING YOUR
PORTFOLIO
EFFECTIVELY

ADEYEMI ADEBANJO

Order this book online at www.trafford.com
or email orders@trafford.com

Most Trafford titles are also available at major online book retailers.

Print information available on the last page.

ISBN: 978-1-6987-0114-1 (sc)
ISBN: 978-1-6987-0116-5 (hc)
ISBN: 978-1-6987-0115-8 (e)

Library of Congress Control Number: 2020910229

Trafford rev. 07/29/2020

www.trafford.com
North America & international
toll-free: 1 888 232 4444 (USA & Canada)
fax: 812 355 4082

CONTENTS

PREFACE

You're interested in making money from the Nigerian stock market and have picked up this book because you want to learn how, good call! The cardinal objective of the book is to do exactly what it says on the front cover—share with you tips and tricks for trading stocks in the Nigerian stock market and managing your portfolio effectively.

Whether you already trade equities or have just made a life-changing decision to start out, either way, this book will help you. It's not just another book—it's a concise book written in a key fact style, presenting only the relevant information about the subject. It's been written to meet the needs of equity investors who want to spend limited time in trading or investing, but want to achieve the highest level of success in a volatile stock market—The Nigerian stock market.

Whatever your trading goal, whether it be short-term trading for quick financial gains or long-term trading for portfolio building, you've the right book in your hands. It will help you a great deal. It presents in-depth discussions on various trading and portfolio management techniques that can help anyone interested in learning the best ways to overcome fear and bureaucracies in Nigeria's stock trading space. It's written in a simple format with no clutter to take away from the actual purpose.

As a beginner in stock trading, this book will hold your hand and guide you through your first and next steps as a stock trader in Nigeria. It's designed to provide you with quick references as you trade stocks and equip you with the knowledge that can help you reduce trade risks, manage your portfolio effectively and bypass societal problems that affect the dynamics of the Nigerian stock market. In fact, it contains all the cutting-edge information to get you started and keep you going.

Having learnt the hard way, this book was born out of my struggles as a stock trader from my salad years of stock investing until the present. With over fifteen years of experience under my belt, I've seen most of the challenges faced by tyros and mid-level traders in the stock market. My understanding of the market will brace you for a successful journey as an investor and stock trader in Africa's largest economy.

Coupled with experience, I've completed practical and extensive research on the workings and ethics of the stock market. This book is a by-product of that demanding research. A lot of investors have had awful experiences in the past where they felt that the market didn't provide the returns they were expecting. This book shares information on how you can navigate the market with little effort, be better prepared to participate quite effectively, and maximise your ROI.

The internet is proliferated with hard-coded and recycled information on how to trade stocks, but I'm yet to see any material that focuses explicitly on the Nigerian stock market and tackles the impact of societal factors on investment returns or how to manage one's stock portfolio conscientiously in the midst of the 'Nigerian factor'. All that is available is bits and pieces of information from various web pages or books that are difficult to put together, hence the need for this book.

This book assumes that you're computer literate—having the most basic knowledge and skills to operate a computer and access a web application on the internet. A lot of the trading tips uncovered require accessing information on the web. Trade processes in Nigeria have been digitised, so it's impossible to talk about trading stocks or managing one's portfolio effectively without making reference to online resources. The book is garnished with a list of useful web addresses and other online resources that will point you in the right direction. You can find these resources at the back of the book.

Please be aware that by the time you lay hands on this book, some of the specified web addresses may be obsolete due to website updates and changes, but nonetheless, you'll be able to search online to find the current information and web pages. I have made a diligent effort to present search keywords that will help you find information quickly and easily.

The book has been painstakingly prepared, and every effort has been made to achieve the correct language level and to present the essential material in a straightforward, comprehensible and user-friendly manner. Definitions of key terms appear in emphasis for your attention. The definitions are simple and jargon-free.

For those who are yet to invest in the Nigerian stock market, I hope this book will further strengthen your interest in equity investment in this part of the world; and for those who have started out, I hope it will help you achieve greater success in trading stocks and in managing your portfolio effectively.

INTRODUCTION

O kay, so you want to be an equity investor—buying company equities at low prices and selling at higher prices, earning dividends from company profits—or perhaps you just have a torrid passion for understanding the economic module of the Nigerian stock market. Well, just hang on to your horses! You've made the right decision.

Behind every stock purchased, there's a company. How much do you know about the company? How much of its operations are you familiar with? Some ask: 'What am I investing in when I commit my money to the stock market? How volatile is the Nigerian stock market? Can the stock market meet my investment goals? Can I invest safely in Nigeria?' These are some of the questions posed by traders making their foray into stock trading and those sizing up the potentials of the Nigerian stock market. The questions are by all means valid and will be addressed as you read on.

The Nigerian stock market is a lucrative and competitive one with generous rewards. Before you turn your fortunes over to a stockbroker or brokerage, it's a good idea for you to organise yourself a little. While the stockbroker can be your hand-holder and guide you through the processes, you'll be doing yourself a lot of good by obtaining some basic knowledge of how things work.

Your investment portfolio must be remunerative; otherwise, I don't see any reason why you would want to invest in stocks. The stock market is a risky market, but it can also be very rewarding, so this makes the market volatile.

My father was a perfect example of what stock trading was in Nigeria way back then. I have a long memory of how he traded stocks in his heyday and managed his investments. As a little boy, watching him hanker for every bit of information, trawling through the pages of business newspapers, journals and financial reports of companies he invested in was daunting. The first errand he sent me every blessed morning was to buy him a business newspaper. At prime time, he would sit glued to his rocking chair in front of our dingy black and white television, paying keen attention to financial or business news. He relied heavily on every bit of information he could find to make the correct decision as in what companies to invest his money and the quantum of funding that each investment would require.

The moment he found that killer information he was looking for, he would pick up the phone and chase his stockbroker to place 'buy' or 'sell' orders. Oftentimes, I would travel with him over Third Mainland Bridge from Lagos Mainland, where we lived, to the Island, where most registrars were based in those days, going from one registrar's office to the other to sign or submit all sorts of documentation. If he wasn't signing documents, he would be collecting new dividend warrants or revalidating stale ones. The process was manual and laborious. My father was a shrewd equity investor who successfully built a portfolio that consistently provided him with a healthy retirement income.

Not yet mainstream, but technology is rapidly evolving in this part of the world. As a result, the way equities are traded has become more modern and effortless. With a computer or a smartphone with access to the internet and a little investment in small pieces of equipment like a printer and scanner, you can do end-to-end stock trading from anywhere in the world. My father passed on a stock-investing legacy, but I don't trade or manage my investments the way he did. These days, one can open a bank and stockbroking account remotely, place 'buy' and 'sell' orders online, set up an e-dividend mandate, update one's personal details with stockbrokers and registrars on the web, track market information on the internet and analyse company financials using online tools—the list is too great to be catalogued.

The Nigerian stock market has become less bureaucratic in recent years. Various processes and schemes set up by the Securities and Exchange Commission (SEC) and the Nigerian Stock Exchange (NSE) have helped make the market more investor-friendly. While societal factors are inextirpable, recent policies have given the Nigerian stock market a brand-new look.

Various registrars and stockbrokers have also set up online portfolio management portals that allow investors to manage their investments online. The Central Securities Clearing System (CSCS) has an encompassing online portal where traders can view all their equity investments in one go. A lot has been happening, so it's an exciting time to be a stock trader in Nigeria.

If you require additional tips to help you trade stocks or manage your stock portfolio efficiently, subscribe to my newsletter by sending an email to **ade@equity-ideas.com**.

You can get help or guidance with choosing a stockbroker, setting up a stockbroking account, opening a bank account from abroad, setting up a CSCS online account, trading stocks online, trading with tools, managing portfolios, etc.

Also, don't hesitate to contact me for corrections, questions and suggestions via email.

You can also write to me at:

Equity Ideas,
PO box 6222,
Ikeja,
Lagos State,
Nigeria.

ABOUT THE AUTHOR

Adeyemi 'Ade' Adebanjo has been an equity investor in the Nigerian stock market for over fifteen years—with commercial and hands-on experience. His odyssey in equity investment started from a young age, watching his father trade stocks, followed by acting as a proxy for him at companies' annual general meetings. From that point on, he remained single-minded in his determination to continue his father's legacy by trading stocks and actively propagating the ideals of stock investing.

Ade is the founder of Equity Ideas, a consulting firm that specialises in the provision of end-to-end investment advice, and/or investment planning solutions to equity investors, helping them fulfil their needs and reach their financial goals. His working knowledge of the Nigerian stock market has been helping local and foreign investors amass wealth.

Besides investing, Ade is a technology man—a software development engineer in test, with vast experience in working with various test automation tools, frameworks and software products. His passion for technology has made him a radical advocate of improvement and sustenance of the digitised Nigerian stock market.

ACKNOWLEDGEMENTS

This book wouldn't have come to fruition without the encouragement and contribution of some key people—David Ebanehita, Oluwakemi Olusesi, Olujide Adesina, Stephen Awotide, Gbenga Afolabi, Ayotunde Lahan and Adedoyin Bakare. Your unflinching support throughout the course of publishing this book was invaluable.

Many thanks to Kehinde Aderemi and Doyinsola Olatinwo for providing extra support and motivation. The words of wisdom you shared were a source of inspiration that kept me going. Your constant checking on the progress of the book was a real catalyst for its completion.

I would like to thank a caring brother, Femi Adebanjo for the constant moral support and genuine interest in my wellbeing.

Special thanks to Adewale Adeoye for creating the book's promotional visuals. Your expertise is deeply appreciated. You have always let me drink from your pool of knowledge; bravo!

I hope soon, providence will supply me with the resources to show you all my in-depth gratitude.

DEDICATION

This book is written in loving memory of my parents, Adebunmi Adebanjo and Susan Olayinka Adebanjo, who nurtured me and helped me become who I am. You will forever remain in my thoughts.

ABBREVIATIONS USED IN THIS BOOK

AGM	Annual General Meeting
BVN	Bank Verification Number
CBN	Central Bank of Nigeria
CHN	Clearing House Number
CSCS	Central Securities Clearing System
EDMMS	E-Dividend Mandate Management System
EPS	Earnings Per Share
FMI	Financial Market Infrastructure
IPF	Investors' Protection Fund
IPO	Initial Public Offering
KYC	Know Your Customer
NIBSS	Nigeria Inter-Bank Settlement System
NSE	Nigerian Stock Exchange
PLC	Public Limited Company
ROI	Return on Investment
SEC	Securities and Exchange Commission

SMS	Short Message Service
URL	Uniform Resource Locator
USSD	Unstructured Supplementary Service Data
VAT	Value-Added Tax
YTD	Year-to-Date

The Whole Essence of Stock Trading

Stock trading overview

In a nutshell, stock trading is the buying and selling of stocks or equities of publicly-traded companies in the hope of making a profit. With stock investing, huge capital isn't required to begin, so irrespective of income level, anyone can invest. However, the returns expected are commensurate with how much is invested.

If you buy a share of a company, what exactly have you bought? You have bought the right to owning part of the company and its profits. Before you buy a share, you may ask yourself: How many shares are there in total? Companies usually display and make public the total number of shares outstanding and the cost of a unit of share. The total value of a company is its market capitalisation.

Stock is a type of investment that signifies ownership in a company and represents a claim on part of the company's assets and earnings

Market capitalisation is the total market value of all a company's outstanding shares, calculated by multiplying the outstanding shares by the current market price of one share

When the owners of a company need money to expand or restructure, they go public by offering parts of their company to people who would like to become part-owners for a predetermined fee. Those people then become shareholders of the company. As a part-owner, you can benefit from share price growth, bonuses and/or income paid as dividends. Ownership interest depends on the number of shares held by an investor, relative to the company's outstanding shares and the class of shares held.

The company is listed on the stock exchange and becomes a public limited company (PLC), as it's now owned by members of the general public. Think of the stock exchange as a supermarket of companies that are on sale daily at different prices.

A stock exchange is an organised and regulated financial market where securities (stocks, bonds, notes, options etc.) are bought and sold at prices governed by the forces of demand and supply

The main goal of an investor is to buy shares and sell at a higher price than what they bought them for, to realise capital gains. This is referred to as capital appreciation. The perfect dream is to buy a stock and have its value multiply over a hundredfold in a short period of time. Well, if only wishes were horses. In reality, the investor buys the shares because they believe the value will rise in the future, allowing them to sell at a relatively higher value. This positive mindset is key to becoming a successful stock trader.

We usually buy a stock because it's cheap or has growth potential. We also buy because the underlying company offers fantastic products or services or is about to release a new product or service much anticipated by the public or a combination of all these reasons. We trade stocks to make money or to build a portfolio that can produce decent financial gains over a period of time. However, stocks fluctuate in price, and there's no guarantee that the company we have invested in will do well.

In addition to making money through capital appreciation, investors who hold shares in well-performing companies can make money through dividend payments, which are issued when a company distributes some of its earnings to its shareholders. The amount these shareholders receive is based on the dividend paid per share multiplied by the number of shares they own.

Shares can also diminish in value, as stock prices can fall below your purchase price due to macroeconomic or company-specific factors. The longer a stock is held, the higher the potential it has for capital appreciation and for a bumper return, although sometimes short-term trading may give you a higher return. We shall discuss long-term and short-term trading later in this book.

Some major concerns of investors include knowing what stocks to choose, what price to buy at and what time to buy or sell. It's not as difficult as it sounds if you adopt a good trading style and the strategies that go with it. To be a successful stock trader, educate yourself. Having relevant knowledge is an essential asset to becoming successful. When you're educated on the stock market and learn what to watch out for, you'll gain an understanding of when to buy or sell and feel more comfortable making decisions. This knowledge will be acquired over time, gradually.

Stock trading isn't only an investment tool; it's an entrepreneurial activity. It gives a sense of business ownership. It's garbage in, garbage out, which means that what money or effort you put in determines what sort of dividend you get in return or the level of success you achieve.

Are there any benefits of investing in stocks?

Stock investing is one of the most preferred forms of investment because you can use a small amount of money to start and grow your investment. Contrary to popular belief, you can start with a small amount of money and grow your portfolio over time by reinvesting your profit, even if you live on a shoestring. Stock trading isn't a get-rich-quick scheme, but over time, you can certainly make a decent living out of it.

For example, I bought my first stock in an initial public offering (IPO) for a meagre ₦10,000. Today, my portfolio is an assortment of over fifty stocks with a respectable value that has grown over the years through dividend and capital-gain reinvesting. Also, whenever I can afford, I inject more money into my portfolio to average down the cost price of stocks that have dipped in value. Stock investing allows that sort of growth, flexibility and manipulation.

The stock market provides plenty of opportunities, so if you miss one, the chances are that you'll be able to find or exploit another. Opportunities can come in the form of a stock being at the oversold region due to forces of demand and supply, a merger, acquisition or an impressive company result. Opportunities can also spring from breaking news, government support and so on. All you need to do is keep your ears to the ground for market information and invest some time in online research.

Investment in stocks comes with a fair share of benefits:

I. Ownership – A stock is a type of security which represents fractional ownership of a company in proportion to the total number of shares. Investing in stocks allows you to participate in the growth of a company and as a result, grow your money. You'll also enjoy the privilege of being able to vote on certain business decisions.

II.   Liquidity – A stock is typically a liquid asset—it trades publicly with price transparency in an established and organised market, allowing you as an investor to buy or sell your shares or transfer ownership easily due to the availability of a large number of buyers and sellers. An asset or security that can easily be converted to cash is certainly a good one.

III.   Dividend income – Stocks provide income to investors in the form of dividend payments. Not all stocks offer dividends, but typically, stable companies do deliver annual payments to investors. These payments arrive even if the stock has lost value and represent income on top of any profits that come from the eventual selling of the stock.

IV.   Capital gain – The other source of return on investment (ROI) apart from dividend entitlement is capital gain—a gain which arises due to a rise in the market price of a stock. Selling your stock after it appreciates in price increases the total value of your portfolio.

V.   Entitlement to corporate actions – As an investor, you'll be presented with opportunities that can help you benefit from bonus shares, rights and so.

VI.   Diversification – As an investor, if you put money into different types of financial instruments, a stock market investment has the benefit of providing diversification. Stock market investments change value independently of other types of investments, such as bonds and real estate. The ownership of stocks can help you leverage losses to other investment products. Stocks add the potential for rapid gains, helping you avoid risk-averse or overly conservative investment strategies.

The stock market isn't a bonanza of free cash, nor is it a licence to print money. A company's past performance isn't an indicator of future success and this makes stocks turbulent, daunting and highly unpredictable. However, having a robust trading strategy and good market knowledge can help to mitigate or minimise risks. If you want your bread and butter to come from stock trading, you must ensure you put in a decent amount of effort in tracking market information and following market updates or activities.

A company can issue its equities through an IPO or through a rights issue (an offer of ordinary shares to existing shareholders in proportion to their holding). Additional shares of the company can subsequently be acquired from the secondary market.

Initial public offering (IPO) is a process through which a private company raises new equity capital by offering its stock to the public for the first time

Are there risks to consider in stock investing?

As a shareholder, you want to buy stocks at a low price in a bear market and sell at a high price in a bull market, but this may not always be easy to achieve—there are always potential risks.

While shares are considered by many as a very risky venture, this isn't entirely true. If you're fully in control and have a simple and clear strategy of trading or investing in stocks, you can minimise risk to a certain extent. There's no one-size-fits-all strategy for investors since we all have different risk tolerance levels and investment aspirations. Understanding potential risks will help you manage your money more wisely.

Stock investing comes with certain risks. Some of these include:

I.   Price risk – The market price of a stock fluctuates regularly; and as a result, the price of your stock can fall below the price you originally paid for it, depending on demand and supply or due to macroeconomic or sector/ company-specific factors.

II.   Volatility risk – Refers to the fluctuation in the value of a stock, due to the changes in price. Stock prices can be very volatile and as an investor, you should be aware that the value of your portfolio may fluctuate sharply in short intervals.

III.   Liquidity risk – Liquidity risk refers to the risk where a stock can't be transacted in a timely manner. When a company is performing poorly or when the market perception of the company is negative, it may become difficult to convert the stock back to cash. If a company goes out of business, its shares will become untradeable and it's likely that the company will be delisted from the stock exchange.

IV.   Market risk – The entire market can decline, thus affecting the prices and values of securities. This may lead to a market crash. Market risk is usually influenced by external factors such as interest rate changes, government policies, the sales performance of a country's major mineral resources and so on.

Bullish and bearish moments

Every stock market has bullish and bearish moments. A bull market arises when the market is showing confidence, prices are appreciating in value considerably and the number of shares traded is high. A bear market, on the other hand, shows a lack of confidence and prices hover at the same price only to then drop in value. To make money, the idea is to buy stocks in a bear market when stock prices are low and sell them in a bull market when stock prices are high. This is the psyche of a stock trader.

Both bull and bear markets present money-making opportunities in their own rights. A bear market can hit very badly, but the good thing is that its life span tends to be significantly shorter than a bull market's; and if you're properly diversified, you can get through without much adverse effect.

A bear market can provide a buying opportunity to uncover a great stock at a bargain price and increase the value of your portfolio in the long run. In a bear market, the stocks of both good and bad companies tend to go down, but whilst bad stocks tend to stay down when the market starts to show bullish signs, good stocks bounce back to winning ways.

The performance of stocks is affected by several factors, including:

I.   Company-related developments – Examples include new product launches, acquisition of major contracts, the performance of the company with respect to competitors, changes in the management team or substantial shareholders and so on.

II.   Demand and supply – Demand and supply in the market affect the prices of stocks. When demand for stocks exceeds supply, which means the buyers are more than sellers, the prices increase. Conversely, when demand is less than supply, meaning that buyers are less than sellers, the prices decrease. So, the higher the price the investors are willing to pay, the higher the value of a company.

III.   Sector-specific factors – Examples include retail sales, commodity prices, government measures and so on.

IV.   Market factors – Examples include domestic and global economic outlooks, inflationary pressures and actions by central banks etc.

V.   Investors' attitudes or reaction to market news – In the stock market, the emotions of investors are an immensely powerful decider. Positive sentiments can drive a stock price significantly in the absence of financial results.

Stocks can serve different purposes. For some investors, trading stocks adds to their stream of income on a short-term basis. Others choose to build an investment for the future by trading on a long-term basis. Some see it as a retirement or pension plan or simply as 'Saving for a rainy day'.

Equity investment can be really interesting when you get the hang of it. For someone like me, the investment is a fusion of both short and long-term goals. It generates income regularly, however much; and is expected to last until and through retirement. Besides the financial gains, stock trading is really fun. When I log into my online account and see my portfolio of investments on the rise, it gives me a sense of accomplishment and satisfaction. The feeling of "Yes, I am doing something right" creeps in. It's one of the many reasons that I trade.

Is stock investing a gamble?

I continuously interact with investors and those that have shown signs of interest in the stock market and my observation is that there's a popular misconception by millennials that stock trading is a humdrum world of speculation. Some think that it's gambling. Far from it. If you share this preconceived sentiment, then you should not dabble into it until you're properly orientated. You should invest more in your education and understanding of stock trading nitty-gritty before venturing into it. There are investment strategies that have defined a bright-line between equity investment and gambling.

For me, I've been privileged to have understood stock investing and been exposed to the stock market long before I bought my first stock—having been under the tutelage of my father on the high note of his stock investing career. This way, I was equipped and knew I wasn't gambling with my money when I started trading. Even at that, I invested time, money and other resources in acquiring additional knowledge.

Historically, stocks have produced higher rates of return than other asset types, and offer investors greater liquidity, being more easily converted to cash than other securities. If you're saving up money in the banks, you need to start niggling about how inflation is already diminishing the purchasing power of such savings. Interest rate per annum will need to be exceptionally high to keep up with inflation rate and finding a bank that offers such a high return on savings is next to impossible. Stocks are the best protection against inflation since companies can adjust prices to the rate of inflation. Gambling doesn't possess these attributes.

Be very careful when trading stocks so you don't invest due to being emotionally attached to certain companies. Many beginners woefully failed the love test by investing in a company because they love a particular product it produces. I have also seen some millennials buy a stock because their relatives or friends work for the underlying company. These should never be the reasons for buying. You're very unlikely to be a successful investor if you trade or invest this way.

I also failed the love test in my early years of investing. My father was a member of the audit committee of a consumer goods company; so every now and again, the company would send baskets of goodies to the audit committee members. The goodies were the company's branded products. Over time, I became emotionally attached to the company, one, because of my father's involvement; and two, because of the goodies. Guess what, the first stock I bought from the secondary market when I started investing was that company, because its name kept ringing in my head that I disregarded performing any due diligence. No technical or fundamental analysis was carried out.

A few days after I bought the stock, the price dipped into the red. I left the stock fallow for a couple of months, hoping for a rebound, but instead, the price dipped further. I did some analysis by checking the stock's price action and realised that I opened the stock position at a time when its price had reached its peak for a fifty-two-week period, so there was no room for growth. This saddened me. I should have done that analysis in the first place. From that day forth, I have never bought stocks without due diligence and I have since cut off any emotional ties with any company. I buy stocks based on their merits or financial prospects, with a 'no-likey-no lighty' approach.

Stable vs speculative stocks

Oftentimes, there will be questions like which stocks should I trade or invest in? Should I invest in speculative stocks or in more stable companies that have been around longer? If you're looking for a simple answer to these questions, then it really boils down to you as an investor. What is your risk tolerance? For investors that want less risk, which of course, comes with less return, you'll want to stick to investing in more stable companies. If you're a stock market Argonaut willing to take higher risks with higher returns or higher losses, then you'll be leaning more towards speculative companies—companies that are less known.

There are some specifics behind the differences between a stable company and a speculative one. A major one is time. How long a company has been in existence plays a huge role in categorising its stability. Speculative companies have been around a lot less, perhaps only for a few years compared to stable companies that have been around for much longer, usually for many years.

The volume of trade is also a large factor. Speculative companies usually have a lower trade volume compared to stable companies that will often trade in the top 10%.

Behaviour is another critical index. The behaviour of stable companies is predictable because they have a long history and a revenue growth that continues to compound time and time again. The revenue may decrease over time, but it usually remains consistent in its up or down movements. With speculative companies, the behaviour is more haphazard with less predictability of what's going to happen.

A stable stock is a stock that provides consistent dividends and steady earnings regardless of the overall state of the stock market, offering substantial benefit of long-term gains with lower risk than other stocks

Earnings also play a big role. Stable companies typically have higher and more predictable earnings compared to speculative companies whose earnings are a lot less, but some investors are looking for a major growth which is why they choose speculative companies.

Manipulation is also a key yardstick. It's harder to manipulate more stable companies and there's less of it due to them having a large market capitalisation and the splashing of more cash to acquire their stocks. There is more manipulation with speculative companies fuelled by their low stock prices.

Price per share is a factor that cannot be ignored. Usually, more stable companies have a higher price per share. Speculative companies are lowly priced.

A speculative stock is a stock that is a subject of speculation, due to its fundamentals not showing any sustainable business model, but seen by traders as having great potential, whilst offering a comparatively low price and a higher level of risk than other stocks

Many investors choose speculative stocks for one major reason, the potential for growth. Since the stocks trade at a lower price per share, you can use leverage to buy your shares; and when the prices rise dramatically, you can make more money. It's a get-rich-quick mentality. This is what many people who trade speculative stocks rely on. It's a lower price that uses the leverage of buying more shares to break even. The more stable companies offer less return in terms of profitability but offer consistency.

Contrary to popular opinion, there's technically no such thing as a good or bad market or a good or bad stock. It all depends on your trading strategy. You must take responsibility for your trading results. Don't blame the market. Whether you make money or not depends solely on your skills as a trader. You will profit if you follow the direction of the stock price, so this makes it a recession-proof skill to make money.

Not all companies pay dividends and this doesn't mean they are good or bad companies. It could just be that they don't have a strong dividend-paying policy or culture. There are some companies that have a high dividend pay-out ratio, meaning that they pay a large part of their profit as dividends. When a company reports an impressive profit figure that surpasses the previous year's record, investors are attracted to it and as they buy more shares, price increase follows.

To achieve success in stock trading, fundamentals and timing are key. You need to understand the company you're investing in, know what drives their profits or their business module and you should be proficient in interpreting investor sentiments, knowing when people are buying and when they are selling. Once you get the basics right, 'a vitória é certa'—victory is certain.

Why Trade Stocks in the Nigerian Stock Market? What Has Improved?

Ranked as one of the fastest-growing and best-performing stock markets in the world in recent years, the Nigerian stock market is an attractive marketplace with oodles of opportunities and has become a hotspot for international investors who follow in the footsteps of the locals. Nigeria is, to an extent, a challenging place to operate, but her stock market is too fruitful to be ignored.

The market has been macerated with improved policies and regulations that underpin the commitment of the market regulators to service excellence. These policies have made the market as attractive as possible with investors singing a new song. Recent performances have proved that the Nigerian stock market is, in fact, teeming with investors willing to put their money where their mouth is. The market is more accessible to commoners than ever before. The days of elite domination are long gone.

It has become more profitable to invest in Nigerian stocks than those of other developing and emerging markets. The market has potential for high and incredible growth, considering cheaper valuations and higher returns on equity, backed by obvious reasons—there is a plenitude of natural resources, endowments and human capital driving the market, making it a very attractive investment destination.

What has happened to the Nigerian economy over the last few years has presented a bargain-hunting opportunity for a lot of stocks. Most stocks are undervalued with their prices more than halved. This occurrence is certainly not due to low-profit margins or diminished revenues, but more because of sentiments. When sentiments drive stock prices, stocks tend to lose their value on the surface and many investors fail to see the gem beneath. For some of those underlying companies, while there is still a lot of value in their stocks, the prices are falsely undervalued due to reasons not driven by fundamentals.

The NSE, as a preferred listing destination in Africa, features large to small-sized companies from different economic backgrounds that meet and adhere to globally acceptable high-listing standards. The NSE services the largest economy in Africa and this justifies the high ROI in Nigerian stocks. The exchange operates a fair, orderly and transparent market that brings together the best of African enterprises and investors from around the globe.

The NSE trading hours are Monday through Friday from 9:30 a.m. to 2:30 p.m. (West Central Africa Time), during which all orders for the day must be placed, and market participants (buyers and sellers) set current market prices. Investors cannot actively trade stocks outside of the trading hours, but can passively do so by placing limit orders.

The NSE is truly on the leading edge and has implemented fully electronic trading, clearing and settlement systems making for speed of trade execution and settlement. Listed stocks are easily traded and market makers also help provide liquidity. The exchange has also put in place compliance standards that ensure listed companies conform to global best practices.

The Nigerian stock market, unlike other markets, has less volatility to market news; as a result, it doesn't quickly react to such news unless it directly affects the profits of the company and investors. This reduces the level of volatility experienced in the market. Highly volatile stocks are ones with extreme daily up and down movements. Price limits help to reduce potential losses in the Nigerian stock market. The market has an upper and lower limit of 10%, meaning stock prices can't rise or fall by more than 10% daily. This helps investors cut their losses early enough.

> Market volatility is the rate or the pace at which the price of a stock increases or decreases and how wildly the price swings in either direction

The NSE has shown tremendous commitment in recent years in bridging the information gap between the exchange and market participants, knowing that the stock market thrives on information. It makes announcements, creates market reports and trading statistics. It also reports corporate changes and other information about the operations of publicly traded companies available to stakeholders.

Setting up a stockbroking account to access the stock market is now easier and cheaper than ever before. I remember when I made my first enquiries to open an account some years ago, I was asked to cough out a whopping ₦5,000,000.00 opening balance for a standard account. I already had a bunch of IPO stocks at the time, so I wasn't new to the market. I knew I could find a lower offer, which I eventually did after a while. These days, an investor can set up a premium account with full use of an automated trading platform with ₦0.00. The game has changed with the help of competition and higher market participation.

Not only is it cheaper to access the market, but the aggrandisement of the market also means many stockbrokers are now technologically-inclined, setting up best-in-class trading engines in the form of web and mobile applications to enrich the trading experience of investors. Some stockbrokers even have specialised research teams dedicated to helping investors make informed decisions that lead to maximised returns.

When it comes to redeeming capital gains and dividends, banking regulations have ensured that investors can now, within seconds, have their earnings transferred to their nominated bank accounts—right from your stockbroking account, you can transfer your available cash balance to your bank account in a brace of shakes.

A key change in banking regulation that has completely redefined investor experience is the relatively recent introduction of dividend payments to a savings account. What a relief this move has been. The investing public was agog at the idea. Before the introduction, it was only possible to pay dividends into a current account. Dividend warrants were treated as cheques and, as such, were only payable into current accounts.

A lot of Millennials struggled to gain access to current accounts due to the rigorous requirements of opening one. As a result, cashing out on trade profits was an arduous task. I remember having two bank accounts at the time, both of them savings. I could not cash out my dividends directly. I was paying the money into my father's current account until I was finally able to open one for myself.

Thankfully, that's all changed. The SEC woke up from its slumber and liaised with the Central Bank of Nigeria (CBN) to compel all banks in the country to accept dividend payments to both savings and current accounts. This development remains one of the market revolutions of the present decade.

Am I protected in the market?

For those who are holding back on trading in the Nigerian stock market due to fear of being swindled or short-changed by a stockbroker, fear no more. The market regulators have strengthened the safety nets by intensifying their efforts to protect investors in order to increase market participation. Improved policies have ensured that every stockbroker licenced by the NSE and SEC is worthy and qualified to serve you. Of course, it doesn't mean there are no stinkeroo stockbrokers out there or that things can't go wrong, but what happens to you in the event of market infractions?

Investors' Protection Fund (IPF) has been set up to protect you and your investments. You can make your case to the NSE and after a review, they'll take appropriate steps to resolve your issues. This innovation has received a plausive nod from every investor.

The purpose of the IPF is to compensate investors with genuine claims of pecuniary loss against brokerage firms resulting from:

I. Insolvency, bankruptcy or negligence of a brokerage firm of a securities exchange or capital trade point; and

II. Defalcation committed by a brokerage firm or any of its directors, officers, employees or representatives in relation to securities, money or any property entrusted to, or received by the dealing member firm in its course of business as a capital market operator.

I've never experienced or suspected any foul play in my dealings with my stockbroker, neither have the people around me. So, I would say to a high degree that there's transparency in the activities of stockbrokers in the Nigeran stock market, many of whom are dedicated and do their job with probity, giving the investing public an absolute peace of mind. With the level of scrutiny introduced to the market, no stockbroker can blow the coop with your investment. The days of stockbrokers taking the low road to success are over, as those with spiteful intentions now have their hands tied.

As for registrars, in a bid to improve operational efficiency, the CSCS has recently introduced to the stock market, a web application that helps to facilitate automated data exchange, interactions and processing of information between the CSCS and registrars. Before the advent of this technology, registrars could only connect with CSCS through a data exchange application that did not have the ability to automatically process the data being submitted. Things have changed. Now, daily processes regarding the maintenance of registers are digitised with instant validation of all data being submitted to ensure the accuracy of records, and in as short a time as possible. It allows seamless integration with registrar's live data by offering end-to-end and system-to-system data exchange between CSCS and registrars.

The reincarnation of the Nigerian stock market

I can't complete a critical review of the present state of the Nigerian stock market without making reference to the bubble of the year 2008 that led to a massive stock sell-off and eventually became a serious fear factor for those who are now interested in the stock market. In fact, a lot of investors dissed and abandoned the market after the infamous crash that left them unquiet.

Panicked investors scrambled to secure their assets as the market took a severe downswing. Many blew their stack and vowed never to return to the market that left their investments hard hit and sent the NSE index to an all-time low. Some others bemoaned their involvement with the stock market. I sincerely empathise with them. This is the challenging world of equity investment and like every business, a lean patch can be experienced and things can go wrong, making you lose money. We all bore the brunt of the market's frustration.

Stock market index is a way of measuring the relative value of a section of the stock market, using imaginary portfolio of securities representing a particular market or a portion of the market

20

The stock market is very volatile. There are opportunities to make high returns and there are periods when prices plummet sharply. Also, the market is linked and responsive to what's going on in the macroeconomic environment of the country it operates in. So, in Nigeria for example, when the oil price is attractive, the stock market posts an impressive performance. When the oil price is under pressure, the market feels that pressure as well.

Generally speaking, company performance is largely driven by the overall sector trend and government policies. When government policies favour an industry, it tends to attract more investment from big investors as they channel their funds to companies that will likely receive a boost.

Another factor to note is foreign investors leaving the market. The Nigerian stock market has a lot of foreign investors. When many of them decide to leave, because they're selling down, it impacts the market adversely. There are many factors impacting the market that are outside of your control as an investor.

The year 2008 market downturn was a result of mostly macroeconomic factors and also to a large extent, poor decision making by investors. First, the Nigerian economy was in a parlous state and second, a lot of investors failed to carry out adequate fundamental analysis on the stocks they were buying. Many acquired their stocks based on hearsay, buying because their friends and relatives had acquired stocks and told them that "I have only just bought this stock last week and the price has doubled." Without knowing what they were buying, many investors were Panglossian—being blindly optimistic of returns. This made the market creaky and this is certainly not the right way to invest. For those of us that did our due diligence, our efforts were in vain as the market could no longer handle the uncertainties facing it.

Yes, the market had its chips, but the bang is over. The Nigerian stock market has woken up fresh-faced enjoying a nice boomlet. Since the revivification of the market from the crash, things have been on the bright side. The investors allegiant to the stock market are better equipped than ever before, availing themselves of resources that provide quality market information and carrying out comprehensive value-added research before dipping their money in stocks. They're constantly monitoring their investments, tracking growth and following events that could affect their expected returns. Desperate times call for desperate measures.

The rebirth of the market has seen many investors take the bull by the horns by uncovering stocks that will deliver a greater return, starting from the overall macro indicator which involves following the global oil market and then focusing on sectors that will benefit from the trend and finding great stocks within that sector. The performance of a stock is largely determined by the sector group and investors' sentiments and perception about growth in that industry based on general economic policies.

One peculiar thing I have discovered about the Nigerian stock market is that stocks tend to move before news break, unlike many markets around the world where investors are privileged to have access to breaking news before the stock prices pick up. This is attributed to societal factors—there are selected institutional investors in Nigeria who have access to insider information, so before any breaking news, the stock is already over-bought. To this end, I suggest you learn how to utilise technical analysis to pick stocks and buy at the right time.

There's now a plethora of web and mobile applications to help investors conduct fundamental and technical analysis and make informed trade decisions. Equity investment without research or the utilisation of market information is akin to bringing a knife to a gunfight. Never rely on stock recommendations. Always do your own due diligence or research about a company or a stock before you invest in it.

The nascent and urbane image of the market gives indubitable signs that foreign investors are keener and encouraged to keep their equity investments here, helping to improve and sustain the total market capitalisation and turnover of the NSE. The market has a highly competitive tax regime for investors, a zero capital gains tax and 10% withholding tax on dividends.

For investors who have recently rejoined the market, gosh, you're in for a treat! The Nigerian stock market has, without a doubt, grown in leaps and bounds as a major player whilst investor participation keeps growing at both local and foreign levels. Little 'Bekele' has come of age.

Listed companies

The following companies are currently listed on the NSE:

Company	Symbol	Sector
11 PLC	MOBIL	OIL AND GAS
ABBEY MORTGAGE BANK PLC	ABBEYBDS	FINANCIAL SERVICES
ACADEMY PRESS PLC	ACADEMY	SERVICES
ACCESS BANK PLC	ACCESS	FINANCIAL SERVICES
AFRICA PRUDENTIAL PLC	AFRIPRUD	FINANCIAL SERVICES
AFRICAN ALLIANCE INSURANCE PLC	AFRINSURE	FINANCIAL SERVICES
AFROMEDIA PLC	AFROMEDIA	SERVICES
AIICO INSURANCE PLC	AIICO	FINANCIAL SERVICES
AIRTEL AFRICA PLC	AIRTELAFRI	ICT
ALUMINIUM EXTRUSION IND. PLC	ALEX	NATURAL RESOURCES
ANINO INTERNATIONAL PLC	ANINO	OIL AND GAS
ARBICO PLC	ARBICO	CONSTRUCTION/ REAL ESTATE
ARDOVA PLC	ARDOVA	OIL AND GAS

ASO SAVINGS AND LOANS PLC	ASOSAVINGS	FINANCIAL SERVICES
ASSOCIATED BUS COMPANY PLC	ABCTRANS	SERVICES
AUSTIN LAZ & COMPANY PLC	AUSTINLAZ	INDUSTRIAL GOODS
AXAMANSARD INSURANCE PLC	MANSARD	FINANCIAL SERVICES
B.O.C. GASES PLC	BOCGAS	NATURAL RESOURCES
BERGER PAINTS PLC	BERGER	INDUSTRIAL GOODS
BETA GLASS PLC	BETAGLAS	INDUSTRIAL GOODS
BUA CEMENT PLC	BUACEMENT	INDUSTRIAL GOODS
C & I LEASING PLC	CILEASING	SERVICES
CADBURY NIG. PLC	CADBURY	CONSUMER GOODS
CAP PLC	CAP	INDUSTRIAL GOODS
CAPITAL HOTEL PLC	CAPHOTEL	SERVICES
CAPITAL OIL PLC	CAPOIL	OIL AND GAS
CAVERTON OFFSHORE SUPPORT GRP PLC	CAVERTON	SERVICES
CHAMPION BREW. PLC	CHAMPION	CONSUMER GOODS
CHAMS PLC	CHAMS	ICT
CHELLARAMS PLC	CHELLARAM	CONGLOMERATES
CONOIL PLC	CONOIL	OIL AND GAS
CONSOLIDATED HALLMARK INSURANCE PLC	CHIPLC	FINANCIAL SERVICES
CORNERSTONE INSURANCE PLC	CORNERST	FINANCIAL SERVICES

COURTEVILLE BUSINESS SOLUTIONS PLC	COURTVILLE	ICT
CUSTODIAN INVESTMENT PLC	CUSTODIAN	FINANCIAL SERVICES
CUTIX PLC	CUTIX	INDUSTRIAL GOODS
CWG PLC	CWG	ICT
DAAR COMMUNICATIONS PLC	DAARCOMM	SERVICES
DANGOTE CEMENT PLC	DANGCEM	INDUSTRIAL GOODS
DANGOTE SUGAR REFINERY PLC	DANGSUGAR	CONSUMER GOODS
DEAP CAPITAL MANAGEMENT & TRUST PLC	DEAPCAP	FINANCIAL SERVICES
DN TYRE & RUBBER PLC	DUNLOP	CONSUMER GOODS
E-TRANZACT INTERNATIONAL PLC	ETRANZACT	ICT
ECOBANK TRANSNATIONAL INCORPORATED	ETI	FINANCIAL SERVICES
EKOCORP PLC	EKOCORP	HEALTHCARE
ELLAH LAKES PLC	ELLAHLAKES	AGRICULTURE
ETERNA PLC	ETERNA	OIL AND GAS
EVANS MEDICAL PLC	EVANSMED	HEALTHCARE
FBN HOLDINGS PLC	FBNH	FINANCIAL SERVICES
FCMB GROUP PLC	FCMB	FINANCIAL SERVICES
FIDELITY BANK PLC	FIDELITYBK	FINANCIAL SERVICES
FIDSON HEALTHCARE PLC	FIDSON	HEALTHCARE

FLOUR MILLS NIG. PLC	FLOURMILL	CONSUMER GOODS
FTN COCOA PROCESSORS PLC	FTNCOCOA	AGRICULTURE
GLAXO SMITHKLINE CONSUMER NIG. PLC	GLAXOSMITH	HEALTHCARE
GLOBAL SPECTRUM ENERGY SERVICES PLC	GSPECPLC	SERVICES
GOLDEN GUINEA BREW. PLC	GOLDBREW	CONSUMER GOODS
GOLDLINK INSURANCE PLC	GOLDINSURE	FINANCIAL SERVICES
GREIF NIG. PLC	VANLEER	INDUSTRIAL GOODS
GUARANTY TRUST BANK PLC	GUARANTY	FINANCIAL SERVICES
GUINEA INSURANCE PLC	GUINEAINS	FINANCIAL SERVICES
GUINNESS NIG. PLC	GUINNESS	CONSUMER GOODS
HONEYWELL FLOUR MILL PLC	HONYFLOUR	CONSUMER GOODS
IKEJA HOTEL PLC	IKEJAHOTEL	SERVICES
INFINITY TRUST MORTGAGE BANK PLC	INFINITY	FINANCIAL SERVICES
INTERLINKED TECHNOLOGIES PLC	INTERLINK	SERVICES
INTERNATIONAL BREWERIES PLC	INTBREW	CONSUMER GOODS
INTERNATIONAL ENERGY INSURANCE PLC	INTENEGINS	FINANCIAL SERVICES
JAIZ BANK PLC	JAIZBANK	FINANCIAL SERVICES
JAPAUL OIL & MARITIME SERVICES PLC	JAPAULOIL	OIL AND GAS

JOHN HOLT PLC	JOHNHOLT	CONGLOMERATES
JULI PLC	JULI	SERVICES
JULIUS BERGER NIG. PLC	JBERGER	CONSTRUCTION/ REAL ESTATE
LAFARGE AFRICA PLC	WAPCO	INDUSTRIAL GOODS
LASACO ASSURANCE PLC	LASACO	FINANCIAL SERVICES
LAW UNION AND ROCK INS. PLC	LAWUNION	FINANCIAL SERVICES
LEARN AFRICA PLC	LEARNAFRCA	SERVICES
LINKAGE ASSURANCE PLC	LINKASSURE	FINANCIAL SERVICES
LIVESTOCK FEEDS PLC	LIVESTOCK	AGRICULTURE
MAY & BAKER NIG. PLC	MAYBAKER	HEALTHCARE
MCNICHOLS PLC	MCNICHOLS	CONSUMER GOODS
MEDVIEW AIRLINE PLC	MEDVIEWAIR	SERVICES
MEYER PLC	MEYER	INDUSTRIAL GOODS
MORISON INDUSTRIES PLC	MORISON	HEALTHCARE
MRS OIL NIG. PLC	MRS	OIL AND GAS
MTN NIG. COMMUNICATIONS PLC	MTNN	ICT
MULTI-TREX INTEGRATED FOODS PLC	MULTITREX	CONSUMER GOODS
MULTIVERSE MINING AND EXPLORATION	MULTIVERSE	NATURAL RESOURCES
MUTUAL BENEFITS ASSURANCE PLC	MBENEFIT	FINANCIAL SERVICES
N NIG. FLOUR MILLS PLC	NNFM	CONSUMER GOODS

NASCON ALLIED INDUSTRIES PLC	NASCON	CONSUMER GOODS
NCR (NIGERIA) PLC	NCR	ICT
NEIMETH INTERNATIONAL PHARMACEUTICALS PLC	NEIMETH	HEALTHCARE
NEM INSURANCE PLC	NEM	FINANCIAL SERVICES
NESTLE NIG. PLC	NESTLE	CONSUMER GOODS
NIGER INSURANCE PLC	NIGERINS	FINANCIAL SERVICES
NIGERIA ENERGY SECTOR FUND	NESF	FINANCIAL SERVICES
NIGERIA-GERMAN CHEMICALS PLC	NIG-GERMAN	HEALTHCARE
NIGERIAN AVIATION HANDLING COMPANY PLC	NAHCO	SERVICES
NIGERIAN BREW. PLC	NB	CONSUMER GOODS
NIGERIAN ENAMELWARE PLC	ENAMELWA	CONSUMER GOODS
NOTORE CHEMICAL IND PLC	NOTORE	INDUSTRIAL GOODS
NPF MICROFINANCE BANK PLC	NPFMCRFBK	FINANCIAL SERVICES
OANDO PLC	OANDO	OIL AND GAS
OKOMU OIL PALM PLC	OKOMUOIL	AGRICULTURE
OMATEK VENTURES PLC	OMATEK	ICT
OMOLUABI MORTGAGE BANK PLC	OMOMORBNK	FINANCIAL SERVICES
P Z CUSSONS NIG. PLC	PZ	CONSUMER GOODS

PHARMA-DEKO PLC	PHARMDEKO	HEALTHCARE
PORTLAND PAINTS & PRODUCTS NIG. PLC	PORTPAINT	INDUSTRIAL GOODS
PREMIER PAINTS PLC	PREMPAINTS	INDUSTRIAL GOODS
PRESCO PLC	PRESCO	AGRICULTURE
PRESTIGE ASSURANCE PLC	PRESTIGE	FINANCIAL SERVICES
R T BRISCOE PLC	RTBRISCOE	SERVICES
RAK UNITY PET. COMP. PLC	RAKUNITY	OIL AND GAS
RED STAR EXPRESS PLC	REDSTAREX	SERVICES
REGENCY ASSURANCE PLC	REGALINS	FINANCIAL SERVICES
RESORT SAVINGS & LOANS PLC	RESORTSAL	FINANCIAL SERVICES
ROADS NIG. PLC	ROADS	CONSTRUCTION/ REAL ESTATE
ROYAL EXCHANGE PLC	ROYALEX	FINANCIAL SERVICES
S C O A NIG. PLC	SCOA	CONGLOMERATES
SECURE ELECTRONIC TECHNOLOGY PLC	NSLTECH	SERVICES
SEPLAT PETROLEUM DEVELOPMENT COMPANY PLC	SEPLAT	OIL AND GAS
SFS REAL ESTATE INVESTMENT TRUST	SFSREIT	CONSTRUCTION/ REAL ESTATE
SKYWAY AVIATION HANDLING COMPANY PLC	SKYAVN	SERVICES
SMART PRODUCTS NIG. PLC	SMURFIT	CONSTRUCTION/ REAL ESTATE
SOVEREIGN TRUST INSURANCE PLC	SOVRENINS	FINANCIAL SERVICES

STACO INSURANCE PLC	STACO	FINANCIAL SERVICES
STANBIC IBTC HOLDINGS PLC	STANBIC	FINANCIAL SERVICES
STANDARD ALLIANCE INSURANCE PLC	STDINSURE	FINANCIAL SERVICES
STERLING BANK PLC	STERLNBANK	FINANCIAL SERVICES
STUDIO PRESS (NIG) PLC	STUDPRESS	SERVICES
SUNU ASSURANCES NIG. PLC	SUNUASSUR	FINANCIAL SERVICES
TANTALIZERS PLC	TANTALIZER	SERVICES
THE INITIATES PLC	INITSPLC	SERVICES
THOMAS WYATT NIG. PLC	THOMASWY	NATURAL RESOURCES
TOTAL NIG. PLC	TOTAL	OIL AND GAS
TOURIST COMPANY OF NIG. PLC	TOURIST	SERVICES
TRANS-NATIONWIDE EXPRESS PLC	TRANSEXPR	SERVICES
TRANSCORP HOTELS PLC	TRANSCOHOT	SERVICES
TRANSNATIONAL CORPORATION OF NIG. PLC	TRANSCORP	CONGLOMERATES
TRIPPLE GEE AND COMPANY PLC	TRIPPLEG	ICT
U A C N PLC	UACN	CONGLOMERATES
UACN PROPERTY DEVELOPMENT COMPANY PLC	UAC-PROP	CONSTRUCTION/ REAL ESTATE
UNIC DIVERSIFIED HOLDINGS PLC	UNIC	FINANCIAL SERVICES
UNILEVER NIG. PLC	UNILEVER	CONSUMER GOODS

UNION BANK NIG. PLC	UBN	FINANCIAL SERVICES
UNION DIAGNOSTIC & CLINICAL SERVICES PLC	UNIONDAC	HEALTHCARE
UNION DICON SALT PLC	UNIONDICON	CONSUMER GOODS
UNION HOMES REAL ESTATE INVESTMENT TRUST (REIT)	UHOMREIT	CONSTRUCTION/ REAL ESTATE
UNION HOMES SAVINGS AND LOANS PLC	UNHOMES	FINANCIAL SERVICES
UNITED BANK FOR AFRICA PLC	UBA	FINANCIAL SERVICES
UNITED CAPITAL PLC	UCAP	FINANCIAL SERVICES
UNITY BANK PLC	UNITYBNK	FINANCIAL SERVICES
UNIVERSAL INSURANCE PLC	UNIVINSURE	FINANCIAL SERVICES
UNIVERSITY PRESS PLC	UPL	SERVICES
UPDC REAL ESTATE INVESTMENT TRUST	UPDCREIT	CONSTRUCTION/ REAL ESTATE
VALUEALLIANCE VALUE FUND	VALUEFUND	FINANCIAL SERVICES
VERITAS KAPITAL ASSURANCE PLC	VERITASKAP	FINANCIAL SERVICES
VITAFOAM NIG. PLC	VITAFOAM	CONSUMER GOODS
WAPIC INSURANCE PLC	WAPIC	FINANCIAL SERVICES
WEMA BANK PLC	WEMABANK	FINANCIAL SERVICES
ZENITH BANK PLC	ZENITHBANK	FINANCIAL SERVICES

TABLE 1: COMPANIES LISTED ON THE NSE AS AT MAY 2020

Wise Words for Nigerians in the Diaspora

First things first, if you live outside of Nigeria, but want to trade or invest in stocks, the Nigerian stock market is accessible to you. The 'distance' barrier has been eliminated, even for a landloper. Various issues have prevented Nigerians living in the diaspora from fully participating in their own stock market, but in response, regulatory authorities have been fighting tooth and nail to mitigate the challenges.

Generally speaking, doing business in a low-trust society like Nigeria whilst living abroad has been a complicated situation for a long time. The reason for this isn't far-fetched. There are societal issues like finding a relative or friend who is local and can be trusted with money. Various economic problems in the country have eliminated trust from the minds of all and sundry, leaving social trust at a near-zero level. Besides the actual cost of getting things done, extra costs must be incurred to make certain that those getting paid or assigned a task are doing as agreed. It's a messy situation.

Another difficulty is in technology. Technology isn't yet mainstream in Nigeria, albeit this is improving fast with telcos tying up loose ends in broadband stability and affordability. The low level of technological advancement has resulted in investors and businesspeople being unable to make automated online payments for goods and services. As a result, people would have to visit banks or other institutions to make cash payments to beneficiaries. If you lived abroad and needed to make payments for your investments, you're screwed. Also, it was impossible for banks to remotely verify the signatures of their customers. There were no dedicated web applications set up by businesses for capturing, updating or processing customer data in the cloud.

All the predicaments listed above meant that trading stocks in Nigeria whilst living abroad was very catchy and challenging. Non-resident investors involved in the Nigerian stock market had great difficulties in setting up a formidable trading landscape. The most an investor could do was send money home to someone who could help them buy stocks from the primary market via an IPO. IPO stocks can't be traded directly by an investor without first setting up a stockbroking account, a task that was virtually impossible in absentia. It was a harrowing experience for investors.

Some of the other problems encountered by those living in the diaspora included the setting up of an e-dividend mandate, updating residential or postal addresses for the receipt of dividend warrants, dematerialising old physical share certificates and so on. Those who already had stockbroking accounts couldn't fund them. Investors couldn't get hold of their dividend warrants or turn them into cash. These bottlenecks drove investors in the diaspora potty. Life was pretty tough in the investing world.

All the listed investor activities, at the time, required the physical presence of the bearer. The bank would have to verify a specimen signature, the registrar would have to do the same for a change of address and the stockbroker could not open a trading account for the bearer without witnessing a live signature and complying with an on-the-spot know your customer (KYC) policy. The process had a way of grinding investors' gears.

In the not-too-distant past, the Nigerian capital market was revivified. Whilst many sectors of the economy still face societal and technological challenges, the capital market has since taken a new turn and has become the barometer for measuring the country's economic performance.

The Nigerian button-down stock trading culture has been made unorthodox with the digitisation of the stock market. New processes and technological implementations mean that from the comfort of your own home, anywhere in the world, you can dive into the Nigerian stock market. Now, a stock trading account can be set up fully online. Investors' signatures can be validated remotely in a recently created scheme, soft copies of old share certificates can be submitted to stockbrokers via email for dematerialisation and change of address proformas can be submitted online to registrars for processing. To make stock participation even easier, some banks now allow instant online set up of bank accounts. Happy days are certainly here.

What's more, the once entangled market has been unsnarled with new deep-seated SEC and NSE regulations for peace of mind and reassurance. Half-baked schemes have been scrapped and otiose policies have been revamped—putting the destiny of investors into their own hands.

You no longer need friends or relatives back home to help you get started in stock trading. Gone are the days of poor foreign investor participation. With full control of the process now possible, a lot of citizens are taking advantage of this long-coveted opportunity to create wealth. The dark days are over.

Requirements for investing and trading remotely

All you need to trade and manage your portfolio conveniently from abroad are the following:

I.   An online stockbroking account for buying and selling equities.

II.   A printer—for printing off documents sent to you by your stockbroker or registrars.

III.   A scanner for scanning completed and signed forms to be submitted to your stockbroker and registrars.

IV.   A bank account for funding your stockbroking account, receiving your dividend payments and collecting the proceeds from your stock sales.

V.   An email address for receiving notifications, alerts and documentation from your stockbroker and registrars.

VI.   An optional CSCS online account for keeping track of your portfolio.

If you've a mobile sim card registered in Nigeria, you can choose to receive trade alerts via a short message service (SMS) whilst you're abroad. Your stockbroker can register your phone number with the CSCS for you. Once any trade occurs on your account, you'll receive instant SMS confirmation directly from the CSCS. We shall discuss this later in **Tip Eight: Open a CSCS Online Account and Enrol for X-Alert.**

The regulatory authorities have explored every avenue to ensure the proceeds from investments in the stock market gets to the ultimate investors who over the years have been short-changed due to malpractices. An e-dividend scheme has been adopted which allows investors' dividends to be paid directly to their nominated bank accounts. Before the scheme was introduced, there were cases of abuse where people endorsed dividend warrants into the wrong bank accounts, due to dividends falling into wrong hands. With the advent of e-dividend, this is no longer possible. The money from your equity sales can be credited to your stockbroking account or directly to your nominated bank account. Also, you can transfer funds from your stockbroking account to your bank account.

If you prefer to withdraw your proceeds or dividends from abroad, you'll need a debit card issued by your Nigerian bank. Most banks now allow international withdrawals facilitated by the issuance of Visa and Mastercard, which has helped to eliminate the bottlenecks associated with accessing funds internationally.

These days, some registrars issue dividend prepaid cards to shareholders into which dividend amounts due to them are automatically loaded or credited on the payable date. You can also load additional money onto your card for future transactions and safekeeping. This means no more unclaimed dividends as there are various options available to access your dividend payments.

Most online stockbrokers in Nigeria don't charge for account inactivity or bill you any extra if you haven't placed a trade in a long while via your trading portal. So, you don't need to worry about having a stale account or accumulating any fees. You can trade whenever you like. Double-check this with your stockbroker.

I haven't approached my stockbroker eyeball to eyeball, visited his office nor spoken with him on the phone in donkeys! The truth is, I've had absolutely no reason to do so and the process is getting better day by day. All my needs as a stock trader have been taken care of remotely. If things get complicated and I need urgent help, from my online stockbroking account, I can initiate an instant web chat. My concerns and queries usually get resolved there and then, or at most, within forty-eight hours. I can upload completed and signed documents and send them to my stockbroker via a dedicated email address for attention or processing. The same is true for the registrars. Online trading is really great. I know what I need to do and am just left to my own devices.

In addition to an online dashboard, many stockbrokers now have mobile applications that allow you to access the stock market on the go. You can place trade orders in seconds, view live market data and stock recommendations. It will give you full control of the market, helping you grow your portfolio easily.

Several registrars do have an investor hub on their websites where you can keep track of the following:

I.   Corporate news

II. Company reports

III. Annual general meetings (AGMs)

IV. Latest offerings

V.   Company information

VI. Company financials

VII. Dividend and bonus history

VIII. Unclaimed dividends

For investors that have bought their stocks many years ago and have since travelled and don't know the state of their portfolio, fear not, your investments will most likely still exist. If you bought your stocks from the primary market through an IPO, you should have a duplicate of the purchase form somewhere. If someone bought the shares on your behalf, ask if they kept a copy.

If you bought the stock yourself, the next step is a bit straightforward. Send a copy of the form with your share certificate to your stockbroker who will then forward it to the registrar for verification. If you don't have a stockbroker yet, contact one to set up a stockbroking account. Follow the instructions in the section

'How to Open a Stockbroking Account in Nigeria' for guidance.

To ascertain the ownership of the stock, the registrar will first need to verify the stock account by confirming that the signature on the purchase form belongs to you. To do this, they'll need you to complete a bank verification exercise. This enables your bank to verify the signature they have on file for you. If the signature is successfully verified, the registrar credits your portfolio with the shares and sends the details to your stockbroker who will update your stockbroking account accordingly.

The BVN Scheme

Bank verification can now be done remotely, so you're no longer required to visit the bank in person. This is a brilliant innovation by the SEC to eliminate bureaucracy within the market. It's important that you're enrolled in the Bank Verification Number (BVN) scheme in order to have access to the proceeds from your stock investments, as BVN is a key requirement for setting up an e-dividend mandate. In fact, BVN has become the ultimate means of investor identity in the stock market. As a result, the CBN has ordered that customers who haven't completed their BVN registration won't be able to carry out transactions in any Nigerian bank and restrictions would be placed on their automated teller machine and internet banking accesses.

The BVN scheme was introduced to protect customers' transactions and enhance confidence in the Nigerian banking sector and stock market. It involves identifying an individual based on physiological or behavioural attributes, such as fingerprint, signature and others. The customer's unique BVN is accepted as a means of identification across the banking system.

If you're not yet enrolled for BVN, but have a plan to visit Nigeria soon, visit a bank branch of your choice to enrol, when you arrive. Within twenty-four hours of the registration, you should receive your BVN. If you're enrolled but haven't linked your BVN to your bank account, you can do so on the web, via online banking. Most banks, if not all, do have the BVN linker option in their online banking portals. If you're unsure of the validity of your BVN, you can check this online by visiting the Nigeria Inter-Bank Settlement System (NIBSS) website (**search online: nibbs nigeria bvn validation**). To complete the validation, you'll be prompted to enter your BVN and date of birth.

You can also undertake BVN registration abroad at an offshore branch of any Nigerian bank or through the outsourcing partners of the CBN—Online Integrated Solutions (**search online: ois bvn appointment**) or VFS Global (**search online: vfs bvn appointment**). Both firms have offices scattered across the globe. You can book an appointment via their online platforms.

It's a very common occurrence for those living abroad to join the Nigerian stock market through an IPO. While IPO is a great way to join, one must be careful about where they put their money. Investor sentiments can drive up the market value of a stock, particularly with IPOs. When a company goes public, the euphoria and industry hype around this first stock it offers may unjustifiably drive up the value of the stock, and because the newly issued stock doesn't have a trading history, the initial high market price may plummet after a few weeks or months. A good way to mediate risk here is to start by investing a relatively small amount of money in IPO and, as the company becomes more promising, increase your stake in the company gradually through the secondary market.

I see no reason now why those interested in stock trading or investment in the Nigerian stock market but live in the diaspora can't have their feet on the ground here or trade like a local. The NSE is fully operational remotely. With the seamless processes in place, you can now rappel yourself easily into the stock market by taking full advantage of the digitisation of the market.

How to Open a Stockbroking Account in Nigeria

Stocks can be acquired directly from the primary market when there are new offerings by companies. However, to purchase equities from the secondary market, you must appoint a licenced stockbroker, also called a securities dealer, and then open an account with the CSCS. Stockbrokers provide advice and make recommendations to their clients but must have a client's instruction before executing a trade on their behalf. They usually charge a commission for their services.

You may be wondering; how do I actually find a broker? How do I get started? What is the sign-up process like? How much does it cost to set up a stockbroking account? How long does it take to get up and running? In this section, we shall go through the process of how to open a trading account with a broker in order for you to begin executing trades.

Stockbrokers are the only persons permitted to transact business on the floor of the stock exchange. The stockbroker will not directly do the trading for you; instead, you'll give the stockbroker instructions on the stocks you would like to buy or sell for onward execution. After you've identified a preferred and licenced stockbroker who has agreed in principle to be your investment partner, set up an account by doing the following:

I. Complete an account opening form. If you've chosen a smart stockbroker (read **Tip One, 'Choose a Reputable and Smart Stockbroker'**), you usually will be able to complete an application form online on their website. If you prefer to submit the application in person, visit the office of the stockbroker. The online platform guarantees convenience as it will enable you to open a stockbroking account without having to physically visit the broker.

II. Present the required KYC documents. For a Nigeria resident, you'll need the following:

    a. Means of identification (driver's license, national I.D, permanent voter's card, or international passport)

    b. Proof of residential address (current utility bill: electricity, telephone, waste management bill or water bill) no older than three months

    c. Passport photograph

    d. Specimen signature

For a Non-Nigeria resident, you'll need the following:

    a. Valid Means of ID (notarized if non-Nigerian issued)

    b. Notarized recent utility bill (no older than three months)

    c. Passport photograph

    d. Specimen signature

III. If you don't already have a local bank account, open one and provide your stockbroker with the account number. Once your application has been approved, you'll have your stockbroking account ready for you in a brace of shakes. Fund it with a minimum amount— every stockbroker proposes its own minimum opening balance, so check with yours to see what their balance is. It's usually a small amount with which you can buy your first shares. The minimum initial deposit ranges between ₦0.00 and ₦5,000,000.00, depending on the stockbroker. This means that some stockbrokers don't require a minimum balance to set up an account for you. All thanks to a competitive market.

To ease deposit issues, some stockbrokers have integrated card payment facilities to their platform where you can make instant payment with your debit card. Otherwise, you can transfer funds via online banking to the stockbrokers nominated bank account. You can also pay into the stockbroker's bank account, in person. Your stockbroking account will usually be credited within twenty-four hours of confirmation of your payment.

IV.   The stockbroker will send your personal details to the CSCS and facilitate the opening of a CSCS account for you. You will be assigned a unique CSCS account number and Clearing House Number (CHN). The CSCS account number identifies your account through the stockbroking house and will accompany every stock trade you execute, allowing the CSCS to keep a record of all your holdings. Both the CSCS account and the CHN are free to set up. Be wary of any stockbroker asking you to pay for these details.

Once your stockbroking account is funded and your CSCS account and CHN are activated, Yippee! You're ready to start trading online. It can take up to forty-eight working hours to get the whole account setup process completed. I opened my stockbroking account in the era when it wasn't possible to do so online. I had to physically visit the stockbroker's office to sign up so that they could verify my identity and witness a live signature. Once there, I underwent a daunting paperwork completion exercise.

As earlier mentioned, without a stockbroker or a stockbroking account, you'll be able to buy shares, but only from the primary market.

A primary market refers to the market where new shares or securities are sold directly by the issuing company to the investing public for the first time through an initial public offering

To buy IPO stocks, visit the bank advertised as the selling partner, complete an application form and pay for the number of shares you would like to acquire. This purchase can be done without the intervention of a stockbroker. To sell the stock or to buy additional shares after the IPO ends, you'll have to do so at a secondary market. This is where a stockbroker comes in.

Dematerialisation of old share certificates

If you've bought into a company before the SEC issued a directive that all share certificates should be fully dematerialized, you'll need to submit your old share certificate to your stockbroker for full dematerialisation. Ensure that there's some form of evidence that the certificate has been submitted. Sign the transfer form which will be provided by the broker. The broker will then submit it to the appropriate registrar along with the certificate, for verification. The registrar will submit the certificate to the CSCS for uploading onto the system, converting it to electronic format. This allows for paperless trading via state-of-the-art technology. The issue of share certificates is now deprecated.

Dematerialisation is the process of converting shares or securities from a physical paper certificate to digital or electronic format

With the growth of the Nigerian stock market, it's necessary for all share certificates to be dematerialized. Electronic share certificates offer a way to get around the onerous task of transferring shares in your name. It also improves the investors' experience within the stock market, improves the velocity of trading, increases the security of shareholding (forfend loss of paper-based certificates) and offers better turnaround timelines for settlement between the purchase and sale of a security.

After the certificates are dematerialised, the digital copies will be held on file and you'll be able to access your portfolio remotely via a CSCS online account—an essential tool for tracking your equity investments on the fly. It's updated regularly to present the current state of your portfolio at any given time.

Stockbrokers can give you their views of the market or make recommendations. It's good to associate with a brokerage firm that offers research. When a firm offers research, you can read their reports for expert insights into what is happening in the market. You can also look out for market information that can help you make key trade decisions. What does market information do? Market information simply tells you how a stock is performing or how it has performed by way of pricing and trading patterns over the years.

Research tells you how the stock has performed in recent years as well and how the stock compares with its peers in that industry sector. It also looks at the sector as a whole and gives you an overview of what is happening therein—are there government policies that will affect the industry or not? Are there policies that will make the industry more attractive? You need to know. You need to be informed about the market, so you know what to invest in. The market thrives on information, so the onus is on you as an investor to research and acquire the much-needed information and knowledge.

Once you've a fully functional stockbroking account, you can start to flex your muscles in the stock market and build a profitable portfolio that can last a lifetime. Your stockbroker is your investment partner and will play an integral role in your journey to financial freedom.

TIP ONE: Choose a Reputable and Smart Stockbroker

As discussed earlier, to invest and trade stocks in the Nigerian stock market, you need to engage the services of a stockbroker. The primary reason for this is that there are no physical walk-in shops or stores where you can go to buy or sell stocks. Stocks are bought and sold through a stock exchange, with the stockbroker acting as a middleman. It's in the NSE's operational procedures that only licensed stockbrokers can buy or sell shares on the floor of the exchange.

> A stockbroker is an institution or an individual who is licenced to buy and sell stocks on behalf of an investor through a stock exchange

There is a goodly number of licenced stockbrokers advertising their services, so finding a reliable and effective one is a herculean task. It's recommended that you meet or liaise with the broker-dealer firm to determine whether the services they offer match your specific needs.

Some stockbrokers don't have online trading platforms where trade orders can be remotely placed. For me personally, this is a dealbreaker. Non-digital stockbrokers will normally request that you send a signed trade mandate via email with all your trade instructions. They'll subsequently execute your order manually on the floor of the stock exchange and send you a contract note. I honestly don't recommend this manual, non-digital, outdated process. It can't give you what digital online trading offers.

A lot of investors have indeed fallen victim to unscrupulous and bogus activities of stockbrokers, but as the stock market improves in outlook, some indices may be used to help you filter a compiled list of stockbrokers according to your requirements.

You can follow these selection guidelines:

I.   First, find a licenced stockbroker, as only licenced stockbrokers can execute trades of securities listed on the floor of the exchange. In selecting a suitable broker to represent your interests, you should confirm the broker's status with NSE. The NSE recommends that investors meet with the broker-dealer firm to determine whether the services they offer match their specific needs. The quickest and most reassuring way to check the eligibility claims of a stockbroker is to visit the NSE website (**search online: nigerian stock exchange dealing members**). The web page has a frequently updated directory of authorised stockbrokers.

The directory also shows the activity status of all enrolled or licenced stockbrokers. A stockbroker may be listed but have an 'Inactive' status, so choose one gingerly.

II. Once you've identified a licenced stockbroker, ask friends, relatives, colleagues, consultants or anybody with stock market experience about stockbrokers. They'll usually be able to tell you a thing or two or make recommendations. You certainly want to partner with a stockbroker with a good reputation.

III. After narrowing down your list, visit the internet. This is where it starts to get interesting. Basically, you want to check if a stockbroker has an online presence. Firms that put technology at the heart of what they do are more likely to make your life a lot easier when you deal with them. Search online for the stockbrokers on your list to see which ones have a website and a good search engine ranking. Those that don't come up in your search may have little or no online presence. Those sorts of stockbrokers are a "no-go area" in my opinion. Once you weed out those ones, you should have a very narrow and promising list.

IV. Ensure that your stockbroker is easy to contact when need be. It always feels good to get immediate assistance whenever one needs it. You don't want a boorish and insensitive stockbroker that only cares about getting a commission from your trades and not about the health of your investment portfolio. On their website, go to the 'Contact Us' page, check if there is an interactive query form you can fill out. Complete the form by asking a reasonable question and send it over. Wait and see if you get a prompt response (perhaps within twenty-four to forty-eight hours). If an email address is listed on the page, perform the same test. Responsive customer service should be taken into consideration when choosing a stockbroker because you'll need all the help you can get. You certainly don't want a stockbroker that will leave you out in the cold during your investment journey.

V. Next step, from your fine-tuned list, find a smart stockbroker. The reason for this is ineffable. You want to be able to trade online, remotely. In this jet age, this is a key requirement. Unfortunately, not all stock traders satisfy this.

A smart stockbroker is one that has an integrated digital web platform where equity investors can perform a wide range of activities electronically, including live trading, fund deposit, fund withdrawal, portfolio view, inter-member transfer etc.

Ask your potential stockbrokers if they have an online trading platform. To identify if a stockbroker is smart, you'll usually see a link on their website prompting you to log in to your online account. The login credentials will be provided by the stockbroker or you may be able to register online. Don't hesitate to check with the stockbrokers the operations that are possible via the online account. Once you're happy with all the information, you may go ahead and open an account via the website. There should be a link on the homepage provided for this purpose. The stockbroker should be able to fully set up your account within a few days.

VI. Congratulations! Now you've the keys to the kingdom. Login to our stockbroking account and play around with your shiny new toy. Explore and see how things work. Get used to the trading platform. Most stockbroking portals have a payment functionality, so you should be able to fund your stockbroking account directly with a bank card. Go ahead. Fund it. Enjoy!

I could have easily recommended to you some stockbrokers that I think are doing well and satisfy the requirements described above, but I intentionally didn't do so because I don't think it's a good idea. First, a stockbroker that satisfies the requirements right now may not do so in future, so by the time you're reading this—the stockbroker may no longer be relevant. Second, it's a good idea for you to go through the selection process and understand how things work by yourself. Performing that litmus test will help build your confidence.

Transferring from one stockbroker to another

The NSE has done well in providing an efficient, transparent and well-regulated marketplace, but a situation may arise where you're just not happy with the services of your stockbroker, for whatever reason. It could also be that your stockbroker is suspended, expelled or has since become inactive. Perhaps you're dealing with a stockbroker that doesn't have an online trading platform and you want to move on to a smart broker. In any of the above situations, it's dead easy to transfer your portfolio to a new stockbroker.

To do this, you will need to identify a new stockbroker and provide your CSCS account number and CHN details along with your identification documents as explained already. If you have an online CSCS account, the easiest way to provide details of your portfolio would be to log in to your account and print or download the details for onward submission to the new stockbroker. Once your identity has been established, the stockbroker will facilitate the transfer on your behalf.

There is an informative online dashboard where you can view the performance of stockbrokers. The NSE publishes a "Top Ten Brokers Performance report" every week (**search online: nse nigeria broker performance**). The report shows the top ten stockbrokers in the country using two major indices: 'Volume of Trade' and 'Value of Trade'. The report is very handy if you're looking for a reputable stockbroker or like to know the leading stockbroking firms in Nigeria week-in-week-out. Some brokers consistently appear on the list and this is a good sign. Statistically, the top ten Stockbrokers for any given period are responsible for more than 60% of the total stock value for that period. This is a robust index for selecting a stockbroking firm.

If you choose to deal with a reputable and smart stockbroker, then you're on a promising path to success in the stock market. It's a good start indeed. You need an investment advisor that will not only offer you advice on how to invest, grow and manage your money, but also make your life easier as an investor. Get enlightened as much as possible before you open your stockbroking account.

TIP TWO: As a Newbie, Start With Penny Stocks or Consider Mutual Funds if You Are Unable to Trade

P enny stocks are small equities with relatively lower prices. From the Nigerian stock market perspective, penny stocks are those valued at prices up to ₦5.00. They are usually small-capitalisation (small-cap) stocks that provide opportunities for investors to make money quickly in terms of capital appreciation or better returns in terms of dividend or bonus issues.

If you're new to the stock market, it's an amazing idea to begin your stock trading journey with penny stocks. But why should you consider starting out with penny stocks? What benefits are there for you?

Penny stocks trade at low prices and as such, are affordable to every intending investor, thereby bridging the gap between the affluent and the low-income earners who now can secure their future as well. The logic behind penny stocks is that with a little amount of money, you can own larger shares easier than you would be able to if investing in large-capitalisation (large-cap) stocks. With whatever money you have in your wallet, penny stocks are more readily affordable than their large-cap counterparts. These stocks give you the opportunity to be an active player in the stock market against the age-long belief that the market is strictly for those with huge investment power or ability.

Trading penny stocks offers investors more room for growth and a higher tendency for a great ROI. Buying and holding shares when the company is still small could pay off if it grows and its share price increases in value. If the company performs, it could eventually move from small-cap to large-cap as time goes by. This type of stock is ideal for investors on small and moderate budgets, who don't want to get their fingers burnt with capitalised stocks.

Penny stocks are often able to increase in price at a faster rate than large-cap stocks. For example, it's much easier for a penny stock priced at ₦1.00 to double to ₦2.00 over a period of time than it is for a blue-chip stock priced at ₦800.00 to double ₦1,600.00 over the same period. Therefore, penny stocks have the potential to deliver higher growth potential and greater capital appreciation. The reason for this is because small-cap companies have an advantage over large-cap ones during the expansion phase, and as a result, their stock prices will rise along with the companies' growth.

While large-cap stocks are usually followed closely by equity research analysts, penny stocks typically have minimal analyst coverage and are less known. With less attention and publicly available financial, statistical and historical information, it's more difficult to conduct a thorough analysis of the market's cheapest stocks. For this reason, it's more common for penny stocks to be inefficiently priced, or not reflective of the underlying firms' intrinsic values. Therefore, penny stocks are sometimes rare gems that are often undervalued.

Of course, like large-cap stocks, penny stock trading does come with its own risks. It can be a double-edged sword. The same way the price can rise sharply, it can also dip. You will have to ensure you do your fundamental checks or due diligence to avoid buying dead penny stocks. To have a better understanding of how to do these checks, refer to **Tip Four: 'Trade With Tools'**.

Are mutual funds worth the investment?

Not everyone has the intestinal fortitude necessary to survive in the world of stock trading. For beginners who are keen on investing in the stock market but don't have the time to analyse stocks or the patience to read financial statements and hanker for market information, all hope isn't lost. Instead of using trial and error methods, you may consider engaging the services of stock market professionals who can trade on your behalf. Many of these professionals have a verifiable record of churning out positive returns.

How does this work? The professionals are called fund managers. To start with, you'll sign up with a fund manager and deposit some capital. The capital from several investors like yourself is pooled together into what is called a mutual fund. The fund aims to achieve medium to long-term capital appreciation through investment in equities with a focus on a portfolio of stocks listed on the floor of the NSE, in order to produce capital gains and income for the investors.

Resources pooled through subscription are invested leveraging on the fund's size and expertise of the fund manager to grow wealth over a medium to long-term horizon to achieve a positive risk-adjusted return. The profit derived from the diversified pool of investments is then shared amongst the investors, annually or semi-annually or as stipulated in the fund prospectus.

A mutual fund is a professionally managed investment fund made up of a pool of funds collected from numerous investors for the purpose of investing in securities

One of the key benefits of investing in mutual funds is that it gives you the opportunity for your investments to be professionally managed by fund managers with the expertise for investment research, due diligence, analysis, and asset selection. The experts monitor the performance of your portfolio with a view of ensuring that your investment goals are achieved. Where required, fund managers engage in portfolio rebalancing or strategy change to keep the investments in line with the anticipated outcome.

Don't confuse a stockbroker with a fund manager. A stockbroker will, on your behalf, and in accordance with your instructions buy and/or sell stocks of your choice. You'll monitor the performances of the stocks independently. In a mutual fund, however, the fund manager determines which investment decisions to make rather than taking your instruction on what shares should be bought or sold. The shares you buy in the mutual fund are those of the fund and not directly those of the companies quoted on the stock exchange or indeed any quoted investments.

A fund manager is someone responsible for managing an investment fund or implementing a fund's investing strategy on behalf of investors who have pooled funds together for the purpose of realising financial gains through a portfolio of investments, for example, mutual fund

Similar to stockbrokers, fund managers will charge you for helping you invest your money. They sometimes charge you fees upfront when you invest and also charge you a fee when they make a profit on your investment. Profits are declared after deducting from the revenue, the cost of investments, statutory expenses, taxes and so on. The fees for mutual fund investment differ from fund to fund and as such, cost should be one of the indices for determining what fund to invest in.

Most of the fees charged by fund managers are flat fees that don't change in proportion to differences in a fund's asset value. There's the tendency for small funds to have higher expense ratios than bigger ones, so make sure you study the prospectus of your chosen fund manager to have a concrete idea of not only the gains to expect from your investment, but also the associated fees you will incur.

Like other investment vehicles, investing in a mutual fund is certainly no guarantee that your investments will increase in value, but it's a good way to avoid some of the complicated decision-making involved in stock investing. There's a plethora of benefits in investing in mutual funds, especially as a new investor. Let's take a look at some of them:

I.   Diversification – While some funds are sector-focused, many are diversified. Equity-based mutual funds spread their holdings across various industry sectors, reducing the effect any single sector has on the overall portfolio. Because mutual funds can contain hundreds of stocks, investors are less affected if one security underperforms. Diversification is easily achieved with mutual funds as it's easier for an investment to be leveraged across many stocks than it is for an individual investor to buy into many stocks.

II.   Professional management – Mutual fund accounts are managed by qualified professionals. They invest only after conducting a careful analysis of the performance and prospects of different equities. It's a continuous process that takes time and expertise which will add value to your investment.

III.   Regulations – Mutual funds are required to be registered with the SEC. The fund managers are obliged to follow strict regulations designed to protect investors, so you can rest assured that your investment is in safe hands.

IV.	Affordability – As a small investor, you may find it's not possible to buy shares of larger corporations. With mutual funds, you can get started because of the minimal investment requirements. Also, the cost of trading is spread across all investors in the fund, thereby lowering the cost per individual.

V.	Liquidity – With open-end funds, you can redeem all or parts of your investment any time you wish and receive the current value of the shares. Moreover, the process is standardized, making it swift and efficient.

VI.	Transparency – As a unitholder, you're provided with regular updates, for example, daily net asset value, bid and offer prices as well as information on the fund's holdings and the fund manager's trading strategies.

A mutual fund is profitable but not devoid of risks. You can easily know how profitable a mutual fund is or can be if the fund owners already have a history. Most of the A-list fund managers already have experience in running funds and so have solid track records of their past performances. It's also important that you look at what type of returns they intend to offer to their investors.

For a new investor, one of the setbacks of investing in mutual funds is that it becomes rather difficult for you to learn the ropes of stock trading if you're someone that really wants to understand the nitty-gritty of this business venture, but doesn't have a stockbroking account that you manage yourself. The best way to learn anything is to practise it. A mutual fund doesn't really give you that opportunity. However, if you're really hellbent on wanting to make money from the stock market without wanting to do it yourself, then mutual fund investing is definitely the way to go.

In the 'Online Resources' section of this book, you'll find a list of selected equity-based mutual funds with fund managers that have prided themselves in their performances and results. Some of them have in recent times posted impressive results that are above the NSE index.

TIP THREE: Trade Online

Once you've funded your online stock trading account, you can start trading and building an equity portfolio. You don't need to be a financial expert or have a degree in business to start trading. Many stockbrokers have a trading platform that is a wellspring of ideas. A stock trading platform is naturally designed to provide round the clock access to great tools and a robust body of research as well as up-to-date market analysis. It aims to provide you with the knowledge you need to make informed investment decisions while you invest and make money on your own, wherever you are. Thanks to the wizardry of modern technology.

Investors who are tenderfeet will inevitably be nervous at the sight of their stockbroking account as things may be a bit beyond their ken—not knowing where to start. So, if you're completely new to stock trading, you'll need to take baby steps. Don't rush things. Get the hang of how things work before you buy stocks. You particularly need to understand how the online trading platform works and how it can help you achieve your goals.

One of the fastest-growing markets online is the stock market. If you've grown accustomed to the orthodox methods of exchanging stocks, then having quite a few hesitations with buying and selling stocks online is understandable and quite normal. What you should know is that online trading can be very efficient and beneficial to you as an investor.

At the time I started trading stocks a number of years ago, I didn't have full access to online trading, so my first stocks were manually acquired via an IPO, however, with online trading, possibilities now exist to execute trades with a few clicks and no direct communication is needed with my stockbroker. Online trading has eradicated the chances of wrong trade executions due to miscommunication or misinterpretation, which was a common occurrence.

Time is a very essential element in trading stocks. Online trading facilitates instantaneous transactions and is without doubt, the fastest way to execute a stock trade. The trading platform is like having my stockbroker with me on the go. I can simply make anywhere my trading floor and trade when I want—during trading hours. With the rise of the internet in Nigeria, stockbroking has been fully digitised. The 'buy' and 'sell' orders submitted by investors are processed electronically by computers, as opposed to humans. Stock trading has progressed to an era of unexampled capabilities.

In addition to having access to an effective online training platform, you need the skills and the patience to select the right stocks to invest in. These skills will be acquired over time, after your baby steps.

Online trading is the act of buying and selling stocks through a stockbroker's internet-based trading platform, using a computer or a mobile device

It's pertinent to point out that online trading requires some knowledge of how to use a computer. Basic computer knowledge, particularly to perform actions like opening a browser, checking emails, uploading and downloading documents, installing basic software products, logging into web applications, opening a website, navigating between multiple web pages or applications, printing a document etc. are essential. If you don't have the knowledge, I advise you to lay yourself out by building your computer skills first before attempting to trade online. You will need these skills to be a successful online trader.

Besides your computer skills, another important resource is the internet. Your computer or mobile device will have to be connected to the internet for you to be able to access the trading platform or trade online.

Online trading will give you an unprecedented trading experience. It improves the speed at which transactions are executed and settled. It also eliminates the copying and filing of paper-based orders. When you place an online order, within seconds and without human intervention, your trading platform connects to a back-end engine or database that checks for the best price by searching the market. The entire process is automated and as quick as a bunny.

Contacting your stockbroker to place trade orders can be time-consuming. If you think about it, there are several investors calling the same stockbroker to place trade orders which may result in the broker not having enough time on your call to fully understand your requirements and give you the best guidance or support. With online trading, you take control of your investment decisions.

For your online trade order to go through successfully, your trading account must have sufficient funds to accommodate the 'buy' trade size and value, otherwise, it will be rejected and the system will notify you of this. When a 'sell' order is executed, you can have the funds from the transaction credited to your stockbroking account there and then. Funds from a 'buy' transaction would be instantly debited to your account.

Online trading platforms have a blend of features and a continuum of functionalities designed to enable you to monitor your portfolio performance more closely and conduct an independent technical analysis. Depending on the type of account or vendor that you have, the following is a wide range of things you can do via a stockbroking account in addition to buying and selling stocks:

- Follow daily market updates like corporate actions, corporate benefit triggers, economic briefs etc.
- Monitor stock prices in real-time
- Evaluate profit and loss in real-time
- Deposit funds using your bank cards
- Withdraw funds by transferring money from your trading account directly to your bank account
- View the volume of transactions done on a particular stock
- Access your current cash position
- Perform an inter-member stock transfer
- View the total value of your holdings and history of all your completed trade transactions
- View/Print your cash statement of account and portfolio valuation
- Check the status of your deposited share certificates
- Download market research reports
- View stock recommendations

Online trading particularly favours active traders who want to make quick and frequent trades and who trade in bulk on leverage. The platform presents you with the freedom, flexibility, and opportunities to maximise your earnings. The ability to monitor stock prices in real-time means that you can react instantly to a favourable share price increase. This instant reaction is impossible when trading offline.

One fine advantage of using an online platform is that you can cancel your order as long as it hasn't been executed. Let's look at an example: Company Y currently trades at ₦5.00 per share and you place a 'sell' order at a limit price of ₦5.20 (during trading hours).

Soon after, if the share price rises to a price higher than the limit price, say ₦5.40 and your order hasn't been executed for any reason (this does happen sometimes), you can instantly cancel the trade and place a new 'sell' order for ₦5.40 or higher, giving you more control over your earning potentials. You're far more unlikely to achieve this with offline trading.

Another exclusive benefit of trading online is that, from your account, you can see the bid prices at which some other investors want to buy the same stock you're considering. The information is particularly useful when placing limit orders. It gives you an idea of what price to set for your order and how competitive and in-demand the stock is that you're considering to buy. In addition to seeing bid prices, you're also able to view the offer prices at which investors are willing to sell, giving you an idea of the stock's performance.

BIDS   OFFERS

Price	Quantity	Count
12.5	1241	2
12.3	100500	2
12.2	300	1
12.1	820	2
12	3036100	15
11.9	5000	1
11.65	1000	1
11.6	5000	1
11.5	208250	6
11.2	5000	1
11.1	100000	2
11.05	150000	2
11	385800	6

Price	Quantity	Count
12.7	1000	1
12.85	19500	1
13	10200	2
13.3	39918	1

FIG. 1: BIDS AND OFFERS FROM OTHER INVESTORS
DISPLAYED IN A STOCK TRADING PLATFORM

If your order is rebuffed, you can see the rejection reason in your online account and can make a quick amendment, usually by placing a new order. This flexibility cannot be achieved with offline trading.

It's very possible to make an instant profit on a trade. You can buy a stock and the price can appreciate or depreciate within the next few seconds or minutes. The easiest way to observe such an instant price change is when you trade online. After the purchase, if you immediately refresh the web page that displays your portfolio, you'll observe any price change. If there is a capital appreciation, you can cash out instantly.

One of the ways to make money in the stock market is the right timing. Online trading helps in this regard as you can monitor price movements and do technical analysis on the stock in order to determine the best entry price. In addition, you can rest assured of ease and transparency as you see all your transactions in real-time and monitor your portfolio on the fly. Some stockbrokers also have mobile trading apps that you can download on your phone or tablet. If your stockbroker offers this service, take advantage of it. These things make equity investment an idyllic experience.

With the many benefits that online stock trading can give you, trading stocks through the internet is a great way to participate in the stock market. Not only are things made easier for you, but you'll also save so much time and money, as well as gain more control of your investments. Be a smart investor, trade at your convenience. Take advantage of online trading possibilities. Go digital.

TIP FOUR: Trade With Tools

S tock trading requires that investors keep up to date with the performances of companies they have invested in, the companies' business model, revenue, net income, profit margin, dividend history, debt-to-equity ratio, price-to-earnings ratio, growth opportunity and what gives them a comparative advantage over their competitors. Keeping track of all these can answer questions like the following: Is a company's revenue growing? Is the company able to manage the cost of sales? Is the profit before and after tax growing? Is the return on equity growing while debt to equity declines?

The best stocks to buy are not stocks that are rising sharply based on temporary news but the ones with sustainable best-in-class gains, robust and improving financial metrics that support strong price growth. Online tools can help you explore these metrics without manually having to perform complex financial ratio analysis. Speculation isn't an investment strategy, so you should make trade decisions based on research and information. Online tools are there to help you make informed decisions. A good source of information is usually the company's annual financial report which tells you the general state of the company at the end of the last fiscal year.

Let's face it—we all know how challenging it is, in the midst of our tight schedules, to read numerous financial reports before every trade. In addition, before the next financial report is produced, a lot could have happened after the last publication, meaning a financial report isn't dynamic enough to present real-time company information.

Online tools can help you with the much-needed dynamic market information required for making informed investment decisions. The tools process and analyse stock market data and present them in a way that is easy for you to understand. All in one place, you can easily find stocks based on different performance indicators, index groups, NSE compliance status, and so on. The tools capture the current state of the market in real-time and present the fundamentals and performance metrics of each listed company, giving you an outlook of the overall market trend to ascertain investors' sentiments.

But why should we do technical analysis before purchasing a stock? There are a number of reasons why it's a useful exercise:

I.   It tells us whether the market is going up or down.

II.   It tells us whether the up or downtrend of the market is strong or weak.

III.   It reveals to us whether the market is about to reverse to the other side of the divide— if it's going up you will get to know when it's about to go to the downside and vice versa.

Technical analysis is a process of evaluating a stock by using its previous prices, patterns or trade volumes to predict the future direction of the stock price

Online, you can track company financial results for different times of the year, for example, First Quarter (Q1), First Half (H1), Fiscal Year (FY) etc. Before buying a stock, I always take a critical look at the price chart—how low and how high the stock price has gone in the past year, for example. For the current quarter, I check the total volume traded so far, the total value, the average price etc. Quarterly reports are a pivotal piece of information for every investor and so should be your good friend.

Of course, which stocks to buy will depend on individual goals and plans since everyone is at a different point in time and has a different amount of capital, so it can be quite difficult to decide sometimes. If you want a keep-it-simple approach, I will say get a good stable company that may not necessarily have the most value appreciation but has a long and stable dividend history. So if you're investigating some potential companies, identify which ones have a strong reputation for paying consistently. Just like blue-chip stocks, penny stocks can also fall into this category.

A quick way of finding this information is to do an online search. Some companies or their registrars display this information on their website. Search the name of the company or the registrar followed by the text 'dividend history, for example, 'Nestle Nigeria plc dividend history'. Some useful results should come up that can lead you to the webpage showing the much-needed information.

Registrar is an institution that is responsible for the keeping of records of shareholders, ensuring that the number of shares outstanding in the market matches the number of shares authorised by the company

A good place to start with the use of tools is the NSE website. The site produces a very handy weekly market report. The reports are a detailed summary of trading activities on the floor of the exchange, including the top traded equities, price changes, company financials and corporate actions. The report groups index movement by market sectors, allowing you to clearly identify the sectors recording the best positive performance and those with the least volume interest. This information will give you an idea of where to invest your money. Once you have identified the profitable sectors, you can go ahead and research which companies in these sectors are the big players.

A corporate action is any event or activity initiated by a company that impacts its share price or stakeholders or brings material change

A more concrete option is the use of some third-party tools. Many of today's independent research firms offer investors an impressive suite of tools to help optimize trades. The tools provide users with real-time market data with the availability of various technical indicators to analyse the trend and momentum of the market. One such tool that has been very good and consistent in providing this information in the last couple of years is the capital assets company research tool (**search online: capital assets nigeria**)

Once on the capital assets website, navigate to the company research webpage and select the company you would like to research. You'll then be presented with useful information about the company's historical performance and financial data. You can view stock prices over a period of time, the number of trades, volume etc. You can also search to find the highest and lowest stock prices over a specified period.

Another good tool I use very much is the Easykobo platform (**search online: easykobo nigeria**). At a single glance, you can view the last-traded price for a stock, volume, trade value, fifty-two-week high/low etc. The platform is embedded with a stock comparison tool that lets you compare the market information for multiple stocks. This is particularly helpful if you're considering buying into multiple companies in the same period. If you prefer to compare stocks by industry, instead of individually, the comparing tool lets you do this also, allowing you to view the analytics of all stocks from a particular industry in one search. The platform has a 'My Stocks' tool that lets you personalise your research by adding stocks you want to follow as favourites.

Stock Symbol	Last Price	P/E	P/B Ratio	ROE	Market Cap	Revenue	Net Profit	Total Assets	Net Assets	EPS
ANINO	0.25	1.25	5.18	413.00%	6,050,000	406,826,533	4,825,341	NA	1,168,769	0.2
CAPOIL	0.2	NA	NA	NA	NA		NA	NA	NA	0.2
CONOIL	13.15	5.78	0.5	9.00%	09.13B	115.51B	01.58B	67.67B	18.09B	2.27
ETERNA	2.39	1.56	0.24	15.00%	03.12B	173.03B	02.00B	52.22B	13.07B	1.54
FO	16.7	1.79	0.34	19.00%	21.89B	129.44B	12.23B	147.90B	64.38B	9.33
MOBIL	146.5	5.66	1.56	28.00%	52.83B	164.61B	09.33B	70.66B	33.77B	25.87
MRS	13.8	2.53	0.15	6.00%	03.51B	107.09B	01.39B	63.78B	23.48B	5.45
OANDO	2.05	0.43	0.11	26.00%	30.75B	497.42B	70.99B	1,076,22B	267.93B	4.73
RAKUNITY	0.3	NA	NA	NA	NA		NA	NA	NA	4.73
TOTAL	96.3	4.08	1.09	27.00%	32.70B	288.06B	08.02B	116.82B	29.89B	23.62
UNIONVENT	0.63	NA	NA	NA	NA		NA	NA	NA	23.62

Select Industry: Oil & Gas — Compare

FIG. 2: STOCK COMPARISON BY INDUSTRY

For those that love interactivity, the easykobo interactive chart tool is a no-brainer. It's a graphical representation of historical stock prices and trade volume that brings interactive data visualisation to its very best. The tool allows you to view the price action or movement of a stock price plotted over a customised period of time without trawling through a list of companies and prices.

At the click of a button, you can configure the chart to display stock prices for the last ten days, one month, three months, one year, three years, year-to-date (YTD) etc. As you hover over the chart lines, you'll be able to see the stock price for the selected date and a corresponding trade volume in real-time. It's one heck of a tool. Paying great attention to stock price movements at key levels and validating them with trading indicators can help you plot a perfect entry point for a stock.

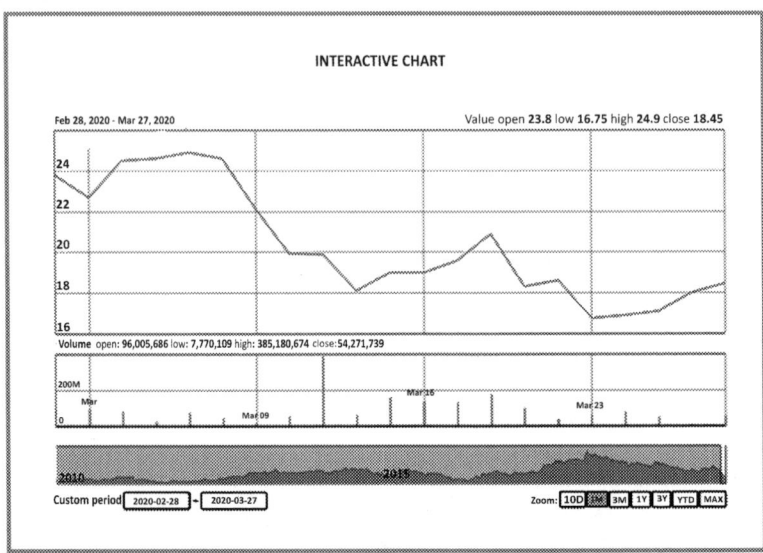

FIG. 3: AN INTERACTIVE CHART TOOL SHOWING
PRICE ACTION FOR A CUSTOMISED PERIOD

Also, some trading platforms have an embedded tool that displays market activities and information as part of their 'buy' workflow. So, when you're completing a buy order, right on that same page you'll find stock statistics. You can initiate a dummy order to view this information before making any purchase.

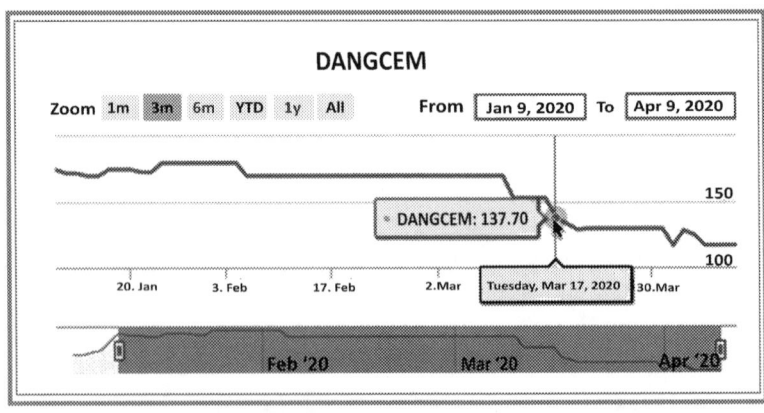

FIG. 4: INTERACTIVE CHART DISPLAYED
IN A BUY WORKFLOW

Before clicking that 'Buy' button, I like to follow this routine:

I.   Check the stock's YTD, fifty-two-week low and fifty-two-week high information to determine a suitable entry point.

YTD refers to the period of time starting from the first day of the current fiscal year up to the present date. The fifty-two-week high is the highest price at which a stock has traded in the last one year (fifty-two weeks) while the fifty-two-week low is the lowest price the stock has traded for the same period defined.

So, why is this information useful? It's a critical factor in determining a stock's current value and predicting future price movement. To put it in simple terms: Within the fifty-two-week range, the nearer your buying price to the fifty-two-week low price, the higher your chances are of making a decent ROI. The chances are even higher when the price falls below its fifty-two-week low. Conversely, the nearer your buying price to the fifty-two-week high price, the lower your chances are of breaking even quicker. Buying at a high-end price means you must wait longer until you can sell at a higher price.

II.   Using a stock or price chart, I compare the momentum and prices of the stock over a certain period of time, say for the last three months or more. Price action lets me view the stock price movement, so I can make informed decisions based on recent and actual prices. The price movement gives information about stock behaviour, stability, liquidity and profitability. It also provides a valuation of the company, for example, if the earnings per share (EPS) figure is increasing and if the share price is going up and outperforming the overall NSE market index. The chart helps me to understand the stock's trend and this information guides in making that buy/no-buy decision. The EPS is calculated by dividing a company's earnings or profit after tax by the total number of ordinary shares. It tells me how much each share in the company is actually earning.

III. After price movement comparison, I analyse a key technical indicator for the current quarter, called volume of trade. Volume analysis helps me verify whether a stock is attracting investors' attention or not. I like knowing what other investors are trading, so the volume of trade is a valuable piece of information that can be used to increase profit and minimise risk.

Volume is the total turnover of shares that are bought and sold at the market during the trading day or a set period of time. A high volume of a particular stock may suggest that traders are showing confidence in it, giving me an indication of how in-demand a stock is and how likely I am able to find a buyer when it's time to cash out. The higher the traded volume for a stock, the higher its marketability. If the demand for a stock is low, the longer it may take to sell it. I avoid inactive shares as it's of no use buying a stock that isn't rising on increasing volume, otherwise, I might be trapped and eventually sell at a loss.

IV. Before pulling the trigger, I check two more pieces of information that are quite handy—number of pending bids and the number of pending offers. My online trading platform tells me the number of bids and offers placed by investors that are using the same stockbroker as I am. If an investor places a bid for a stock, that bid will be added to a queue of pending bids if the limit price set by the investor is lower than the market price. The stock will remain in the queue until it expires. The expiry date is determined by the order term set by the investor when placing the bid.

The system works the same way for offers made by investors selling their stocks. The offers are added to a queue if the current market price is lower than the investors limit price. Those two queues (bids and offers) give me an insight into the market activities of the respective stocks. I can see the demand for stocks, how much investors are willing to cash out and at what prices. This information contributes squarely to my buy/no-buy decision.

Once I am happy with my checks, I can go ahead and place my order with high hopes of making a decent return on my investment. I like to be confident in my purchases. I am not the kind of investor that is easily swayed by stock recommendations. When I receive any recommendation, I follow it up with due diligence before I commit my money to it.

I've found that the best time to buy a stock is when it's recovering from a pullback because it has a limited downside and has more upside potential. As a result, I always like to know the intrinsic value of a stock before buying it and the beautiful thing is that it only takes a couple of minutes to estimate and know which stock has more upside potential than others, otherwise, I may be buying shares at peak prices, leaving little or no room for growth.

A stock may be overvalued at the time I'm plotting an entry, so I'm not usually carried away by a stock's temporary straight gains for a short period of time. Online tools are there to help me analyse a stock's fundamentals quickly and efficiently before buying. When you buy a growth stock that is selling below the estimated value, you have a higher chance of a decent return.

A pullback is a temporary reversal or drop in stock price, to a level of support, usually after a breakout has occurred, resulting in an opportunity for an investor to acquire the stock at a relatively lower price

Fundamentals let you screen for potential stocks that will recover from their bottom prices while technical analysis lets you spot stocks that are appreciating from support levels. With indicators like price action and volume, you can easily scan the market for oversold stocks that are recovering.

For investors that are too nervous to place real trades or find stock trading doubt-ridden, there is a cool way to try out dummy trades to see how your preferred stocks are performing before you put real money in. Some stockbrokers do have a virtual platform where you can do stock trials or practise how to buy stocks under real market conditions without getting your fingers burnt. The platform is usually an exact replica of the stocks traded on the floor of the NSE. Once you become a pro on the virtual trading platform, you can then migrate to a real one. You can register online with the stockbroker for instant access to the virtual trading platform. You can also register for stock trials on a platform like Easykobo (**search online: easykobo nigeria stock trials**)

Investors that have cut their teeth in stock trading don't just pick winning stocks that bring forth rewards, they find the right tools that let them monitor or protect their investment to avoid being cut short on information that would help them in making vital buy/sell decisions.

Fundamental analysis is the process of measuring a stock's intrinsic value by examining the underlying company's financial statements, for example, income statement, balance sheet etc. in order to determine if the stock will make a good buy or investment

Two good open source applications are also out there on the web: investing.com (**search online: investing equities performance**) and bloomberg.com (**search online: bloomberg equities performance**). Both tools can give you a real-time technical analysis summary of stocks from many exchanges around the world, including that of Nigeria. Navigate to the Nigerian stock market section and there you will find the price, performance, technical and fundamental analysis of listed stocks already prepared for you and usable out of the box. The underlying company's financials and historical data are also available with ready-to-use streaming and interactive charts. With these sophisticated tools, you will never be short of stock market information.

There is a reliable web tool that can help you follow updates or get the latest news on your selected or preferred stocks, directly sent to your inbox at customised frequency.

Google Alerts has been designed to help you monitor the web for interesting new content tailored to your requirements. It will automatically send you emails when it finds new results such as newspaper articles, videos etc. that match your search terms.

To set up Google Alerts, go to https://www.google.com/alerts (**search online: google alerts**). In the provided input box, enter the name of the company you want to follow, for example, Oando PLC. The system lets you add various options like how often you want to be alerted (for example, daily, weekly), sources (for example, news, finance) etc. Once the alert is created, you will start to get breaking news that relates to your stock or company. This can help you make key decisions regarding your investments.

Whether you're an experienced trader or one with limited knowledge of investing in equities, using online tools to acquire key market information is a practice that would give you a lot of power in the stock market and help you make informed decisions before you invest in any stock.

TIP FIVE: Take Transaction Fees and Withholding Tax Into Account

S tockbrokers charge a commission when you buy or sell stocks, and this in turn will affect your net gain or loss. Transaction costs are a relatively big factor that you must consider when trading. The fees are basically government taxes and stockbroker commissions. While the government fixes tax rates on profits made, stockbrokers decide their fees as regulated by the SEC. Transaction fees should be transparent and clear, but the onus is on you as the investor to understand what fees you will be paying. Trading frequently could take a bite out of your returns if you're paying a higher fee.

Transaction fees are charged each time you buy a stock and will reduce the overall value of your portfolio. When you place a 'buy' order, you'll observe that your cost price per share is higher than the share price specified before you submitted the order. What happens is that transaction fees are automatically rolled into trade costs by the stockbrokers, as a result, the price paid is always higher than the current price. Stockbrokers do this to make it easier for the investor to calculate the gain/loss on the stock bought, otherwise, you will have a false value of your portfolio's net worth.

> Transaction fees are brokerage and statutory fees charged by the broker and the regulators respectively; when an investor buys and sells stocks traded on the stock exchange

At the time of writing, there is a maximum brokerage fee of 1.35% set by the regulators. Brokers have the discretion to charge a lower rate in order to be more competitive or to promote trading, but they can't charge higher. Don't hesitate to check with your stockbroker what their prevailing rate is.

'Buy' and 'sell' transactions usually have different outcomes in terms of fees.

The table below shows what fee is applicable to what transaction type.

Fee type	Transaction Charges (Buy)		Transaction Charges (Sell)	
	Fee	VAT	Fee	VAT
Brokerage Fee	Yes (1.35% of trade value)	7.5% of brokerage = 0.10%	Yes (1.35%)	7.5% of brokerage = 0.1%
NSE Fee	No	–	Yes (0.3%)	7.5% of NSE commission = 0.02%
CSCS Fee	No	–	Yes (0.3%)	7.5% of CSCS commission= 0.02%

CSCS Trade Alert Fee	Yes (₦4.00)	7.5% VAT ₦4.00 = 30k Total = ₦4.30	Yes (₦4.00)	7.5% VAT ₦4.00 = 30k Total = ₦4.30
SEC Fee	Yes (0.30%)	–	No	–
Stamp Duty	Yes (0.075%)	–	Yes (0.075%)	–
TOTAL	1.725%	0.10%	2.025% + ₦4.30	0.14%
GRAND TOTAL	**1.825% + ₦4.30**		**2.165% + ₦4.30**	

Table 2: SHOWS WHAT FEE IS APPLICABLE
TO WHAT TRANSACTION TYPE

You can see from the above table that value-added tax (VAT) charges exist. Until recently, to encourage investments in the Nigerian stock market and to resuscitate the market, the regulators exempted VAT deductions from commissions earned on the traded values of shares, commissions payable to the NSE and commissions payable to the CSCS. The exemption has expired, so investors now pay VAT on transactions carried out on the floor of the NSE.

So, for every executed 'buy' trade, you need to factor an additional 1.825% to the consideration (the amount you're investing).

Using the maximum payable of 1.35% brokerage fee as an example, if you buy, say 5,000 shares of Company Y at ₦10.00, the consideration would be ₦50,000, but when you factor the total 'buy' transaction fees of **1.825% + ₦4.30** on the consideration, your total contract amount becomes **₦50,916.80**.

The same rule applies for a 'sell' transaction, but instead of adding the total charge to the consideration, it will be deducted from it. So, for example, if you've made a profit of ₦5.00 per share on Company Y, and you're selling your 5,000 shares at ₦15.00 each, it gives gross earnings of ₦75,000. Deducting a 'sell' transaction fee of **2.165% + ₦4.30** leaves you with a net contract amount of **₦73,371.95.**

The concern for some new investors is how to manage or keep track of transaction charges. Fortunately, stockbrokers have made it so transparent and easy to do. When setting up an order, the system will dynamically display the charges for you to review before you hit the submit button. Whether you buy or sell, transaction charges are part of the process. Your contract note will always indicate the charges associated with the transaction. The note is automatically triggered to your email within seconds of the order being completed.

Another kind of fee to be aware of is withholding tax.

Withholding tax is an advance tax payment which is deducted and withheld from any dividend income, for onward remittance to the relevant tax or government collecting authority, against a final income tax liability

There's a withholding tax of 10% which is applicable to dividend payments in Nigeria. The tax is automatically deducted by the company making payments to its investors before the remittance of dividends. After receiving your dividends, you don't have to file an income tax return. This is because dividends are regarded as franked investment income. As such, there is no additional tax due other than the withholding tax deducted at source by the investee company.

You have nothing to worry about when it comes to capital gain. As income taxes are payable on taxable profit, increase in share value doesn't qualify as a taxable profit, hence no additional tax is payable. Dividends from foreign equities listed on the NSE are tax-free in Nigeria. You're not required to file a tax return if your only source of income is dividends.

As you trade stocks, don't forget the all-important transaction fees. They're important to you as an investor because they're one of the key determinants of your net returns. These fees can quickly consume your profit or reduce the value of your portfolio, but if you factor them in from the very onset when acquiring a stock, you can greatly leverage any diminishing effect or threat they supposedly pose to your portfolio.

TIP SIX: Never Sell All
the Shares of Your Stock

$\mathbf{A}$s your stocks increase in value and your portfolio burgeons, it will soon be time to cash out on the ones that have delivered the expected profit margin. If you're thinking of selling all your shares, think again. This is one of those corner cases that require careful thoughts. With the way things are done by registrars in the Nigerian stock market, selling every single unit of your stock isn't a good call.

Given you have a stock administered by a certain registrar and there's an active e-dividend mandate in place. When you buy an additional stock administered by the same registrar, then the registrar should automatically set up an e-dividend mandate for the new stock since your bank details already exist on file. Unfortunately, this isn't usually the case.

The new stock isn't tied to the existing bank details and it remains unclear why many registrars struggle to achieve this. A major consequence of this inefficiency is that you will end up not getting e-dividend for the new stock. In this case, the registrar may send you a dividend warrant, unless you get the new stock mandated.

To eliminate the risk of missing out on e-dividend for your new stocks, ensure you notify the registrar a few days after the purchase. If you have a duplicate of the old e-dividend activation form that you submitted to the register for your existing mandate, tick the name of the company you have just bought into on the form (an e-dividend mandate form contains the list of all companies managed by the registrar), scan it, and then send it to the registrar. If you don't have a copy of the old form, visit the registrar's website, print out a new form, complete and submit it.

When you're selling a stock, it's best to reserve at least one share. This ensures that your account or file is kept open by the registrars, otherwise, it will be closed, meaning if you reinvest in the same company in the near future, you will have to go through the hassle of setting up a new e-dividend mandate. I experienced this, and trust me, it wasn't pleasant.

Assuming you've 2,000 shares of Company Y and have decided to sell your stake. If for example, you sell 1,999 shares and reserve 1, that single share left can serve a lot of good. Here are some of the benefits of the practice:

I.   It ensures that your stock account for Company Y is kept open by the registrar. This way, your e-dividend mandate for Company Y isn't deleted from the registrar's records. If you sell all your shares and your mandate is deleted, you will need to set up a brand-new mandate if you reinvest later on.

II. It ensures that your personal details remain on the company's shareholders list, this way, you'll still get AGM invites and receive dividends (if any) for the little investment you've left.

III. It ensures that the company remains listed in your portfolio and stockbroking account. This way, you'll have easy visibility and tracking of the share price for that stock, letting you see in real-time when the price becomes favourable for reinvestment.

The message is simple—to avoid the bureaucracy of the Nigerian stock market, never sell every single share you own when cashing out on stocks. I can't stress enough the importance of this. It will save you a lot of hassle with e-dividend mandates. You just never know, if you sell a stock, you may need to reinvest later on. If you've kept your file open with the registrar by reserving at least one share of the stock, reinvestment would be a lot smoother.

TIP SEVEN: Buy Bearish Stocks, Sell Bullish Ones

U sually, when people are panic selling, it's because they consider the market conditions to be unfavourable or likely to be unfavourable in the near future. When the market dips or takes an unusual turn, stocks are usually at their lowest. You need to have a robust understanding of timing as a strategy in the stock market and this understanding comes with experience and a willingness to grasp how the market really works. Good timing will help you improve your leverage for portfolio gains.

But why should I buy bearish stocks?

Unlike baby investors, who are usually in a flutter, and emotionally attached to their stocks, experienced investors with consistent winning strategies keep a cool head and don't rush into making quick sell decisions when they see their stocks take a dive. The stocks they buy are not selected by an 'eeny-meeny-miney-mo approach', rather, they are subjected to analytic research and historical performance tests before they are bought. Such stocks bought with so much scrutiny and confidence can't easily be disposed of due to market duress or when prices go southside.

Fortunately, or unfortunately, depending on which side you belong, these experienced investors indirectly capitalise on the fears of the emotional, less experienced investors who sell off their stocks during price falls, making them available to be bought at undervalued prices by those that truly understand the market.

If your stock becomes bearish, don't panic, and don't sell it solely based on that reason—you will automatically lose money if you do. Don't make a short-sighted decision by letting your emotions get the better of you. It is normal for prices to recover and reward early buyers, so a bearish stock has the potential for regaining momentum.

A stock is referred to as bearish when its price has fallen successively week after week as investors react to market news. It tends to fall to a low level where it becomes oversold—its price has decreased to a level where sell orders aren't strong enough to move the price anymore. One often ignored merit of stock prices that are in the oversold territory is that they usually become undervalued and attractive to institutional investors. In a rare opportunity, the stock becomes a potential pick for bargain hunters and value investors, provided the stock fundamentals are intact.

It's a well-grounded idea to acquire additional shares of a particular stock when the market price has fallen below the price you paid for it to begin with—a situation that puts the stock in red. Rather than panic, you should see a persistent bear run at the stock market as an opportunity to take advantage of the low prices and increase your portfolio as the run depresses the stock prices to levels that make them attractive to be bought.

Bearish stock is an underperforming stock whose price has fallen to a certain low level, but with the hope that soon it will recover

For example, if your cost price for Company Y stock is ₦10.00 per share, and the current market price is ₦7.00, your portfolio is ₦3.00, in red. In this situation, don't get spooked. Don't just sell solely for this reason. You haven't lost anything yet. I really get worried when I see investors sell their stake in this situation and I don't understand why. This is mostly done by beginners. The ₦3.00 in question is just a visual loss on paper, not a real loss in your bank account. You will only lose that deficit if you sell the shares at that lower price.

A lower share price is a promising opportunity to increase your stake in a company at a bargain, but you may need to keep the shares for a relatively long time for the share price to appreciate in order to see a significant ROI. This strategy is the simplest way to ideate wealth and a cost-effective one to accumulate it.

Patience is a great attitude to have as a stock trader. It allows your investment to grow, amidst daily price fluctuations, otherwise, you can lose the profit potentials of a perfect stock. To exercise patience, you need to learn the basics of the stock market, understand the key drivers of share prices and how to pick good stocks.

Another apparent reason to buy additional shares when prices dip is to average down the cost price of your existing investment. The more shares you buy at a lower price, the less the average cost price for that investment. You want to drive your purchase price to the barest minimum possible, so that when the stock price eventually appreciates, profit will be higher because you'll have more shares to sell. For example, say you bought 100 shares at ₦20.00 each. If the share price drops to ₦10.00 and you buy an additional 100 shares, your average price per share would be ₦15.00. So, you have averaged down your cost price by ₦5.00.

I'm always excited when the prices of blue-chip or fundamentally justified stocks plummet. I'm more of a low-risk investor, so the bulk of my money is on blue-chip stocks. These are stocks that are perceived by the market as really good quality because over the years, their performance has remained consistent and they have outperformed the matrices by which companies are measured. In the stock market, a blue-chip company is seen as a general outlier and its stock is seen as defensive whether the market is down or not doing great.

Another reason I splash out on blue-chip stocks is that they typically have a consistent dividend yield or dividend pay-out policy, paying almost all their profits in dividends. Also, the swing in the pricing of blue-chip stocks isn't as wide or volatile as others. When a bear market starts to recover, blue-chip stocks usually recover the quickest.

Bear in mind that I don't just buy stocks because their prices have fallen, I still do my due diligence beforehand and hope for a recovery. If I purchase a stock following a solid fundamental analysis, I always welcome every fall in the stock price as a momentary opportunity to buy additional shares and increase my stake in the company.

Investor sentiments in a bear market

During a bearish run of the market, I cut through the market noise or clutter and look beyond making instant gains. I find great stocks by checking the overall market performance and bearish sentiments. I scout for stocks that are showing bullish strength in a bearish period. There are situations where even though the NSE market index is down by a considerable margin in a certain period, a stock increases its value in the same period. Those are the kind of opportunities I look for within a bear market. After checking the fundamentals and analysing technical details of stocks during a market downturn, I usually come up with a handful of potential buys.

You can find bearish stocks almost any time even in a strong bull market. The price drop for very bearish stocks is often quick and deep. Bearish stocks represent an opportunity to make money, using an appropriate trading strategy.

For example, if you buy a fundamentally sound blue-chip stock and a less stable penny stock in the same period and, after a few months, the penny stock delivers a significant price increase while the blue-chip stock drops in price, it doesn't in any way mean that penny stock is better. The only difference is in investors' sentiments towards the stock in the last few months. Investors' sentiment is a strong factor that determines a bullish or bearish market run. It's driven by a combination of financial results, market news, policy directions and expectations, so in its absence, you may be missing out on a big index that could help you identify your next good trade.

As an investor, your decision might be limited to what you know, but sentiments cover what you might not be privileged to know, like insider information or pending market-determining breaking news. Mastering the act of following sentiments when buying short-term stocks is important as this ensures that you're not discouraged when your investment is in the red.

Selling in a bull market

Your portfolio is very likely to be hit by capital appreciation, which is the whole essence of stock investing. We all dream of buying stocks that rise steadily in value, delivering both capital appreciation and a progressive increase in dividends. To not sell the stock when the price has risen by a considerable margin defeats the purpose of the investment. The stock doesn't have any value until you sell it to realise any gain.

Capital appreciation refers to an increase in the market price or value of a stock, measured by the difference between the stock's current price and its purchase price

The main characteristic of a bullish stock is uptrend behaviour. The stock price rises as many investors and short-term traders buy, in expectation of further price gains. The strength of top bullish stocks means that their prices also rise during a market drop.

There's no set rule on when to sell a stock, as it all depends on the individual investor's financial objections, trading strategies, how much risk they can bear and their end goals, but as a simple rule, never sell your shares at a price lower than the cost price. If the market price falls below your cost price, be calm and remain patient with the hope that the market will become favourable.

Greed is a huge factor responsible for some investors holding back stocks that have appreciated considerably in value. Over time, I've learned to not let my judgement be clouded by greed. One thing I do quite often is create a limit order for a realistic offer price. By doing that, I am telling the system to sell my stock at a certain price higher than my cost price. Once that price is reached, the stock position will automatically close. This helps me to eliminate greed.

For a short-term investor who is only concerned about short-term price movements, it's very important to set a profit range and sell afterwards. Greed can be tempting, especially when the percentage increase is above your expected profit margin, but greed can also be dangerous. It's key knowing when to cash out. If you wait too long, you might miss a massive profit. You should set yourself a realistic target that you will comply with.

You will sometimes experience a situation where a stock you've just bought appreciates geometrically in a short period. It's the moment every investor dreams. Be calculative. Sell it. Pocket your gains and find new promising stocks. There are chances that the same stock may drop significantly beyond your selling price in the near future and you may consider buying it again if your fundamental checks give a green light.

In both bear and bull markets, there are always opportunities lurking around the corner. In a bear market, hunt stocks that have reached their lowest low. This bearish period is the perfect time to review your portfolio and consider buying stocks whose prices have fallen sharply. In a bull market, don't be greedy by waiting for unrealistic returns. Take quick advantage of capital appreciation by setting a minimum profit margin and cashing out when the margin is reached. You have nothing to lose.

TIP EIGHT: Open a CSCS Online Account and Enrol for X-Alert

The CSCS is a Financial Market Infrastructure (FMI) for the Nigerian capital market whose primary responsibility is to facilitate the delivery (transfer of securities from a seller to a buyer) and settlement (payment of bought shares) of securities transacted on the NSE. It allows securities to be processed in an electronic book-entry, thereby substantially reducing the time it takes for a transaction to be completed.

As discussed, to trade stocks in the Nigerian stock market, you'll need a user or member code called CHN—a unique number issued by the CSCS to Stakeholders who buy and sell shares on the floor of the NSE, directly connected to the CSCS system.

One of the functions of the CSCS is the clearing and settlement of transactions. Before the intervention of the CSCS, there was difficulty associated with the transfer of shares and the production of certificates for traded securities between stockbrokers and the registrars, leading to numerous complaints regarding failed transactions. In most cases, it took three to twelve months for investors to receive their share certificates, but with the advent of CSCS and the digitisation of the market, the transaction cycle is now T+3 (three working days after the transaction) and electronic certificates are automatically generated and stored.

The T+3 settlement cycle for transactions on the NSE is in conformity with the practice in emerging markets. The circle is facilitated by the immobilization of share certificates within a central location, thus allowing trades to be processed in an electronic book-entry form. In effect, physical delivery of share certificates to fulfil settlement obligations has been replaced by electronic credits and debits to shareholders' stock positions.

With the CSCS structure in place, there are no longer incidences of loss, stolen or the late delivery of certificates. Investment risks have been greatly reduced whilst liquidity of stock has been on the increase, with increased market turnover.

The CSCS has now made it possible for investors to open an online account where they can view and track activities on their portfolios. Your account is updated dynamically as you buy and sell your equities. Your portfolio is a compendium of your investments—you can have as little as one stock in your portfolio to as many as possible, depending on the number of listed companies.

A CSCS account gives you twenty-four-hour-a-day online access to your portfolio. It shows your net-worth at a glance and allows you to view historical information on all your transactions independently. This is important as it helps you mollify fraudulent activities on your portfolio. In addition, you get easy access to your bonus shares immediately after bonus approval and lodgement. In fact, the online portal has an automated engine that can analyse the full range of your portfolio.

New stocks you buy will be credited immediately to your stock trading account but will not show up on your online CSCS account straight away, because of the T+3 transaction cycle. Only after that period has elapsed will you be able to view an updated portfolio. The CSCS disseminates portfolio information by issuing monthly statements of stockholdings to investors, so you can request statements of your stockholding monthly and can download or print them via online portfolio management access.

To register for online access, visit the CSCS website's signup page (**search online: cscs nigeria online registration**) and complete the registration form. Pay the required annual subscription fee and your account will be up and running soon after. The fee is a reasonable and relatively small amount, payable online by debit card or through an online transfer (internet banking). If you're paying through online transfer, ensure you add your CHN as a reference, so the payment can be correctly tied to your registration.

I currently have an active five-year subscription, so I don't need to worry about annual renewal. Also, if the subscription fee goes up, I would not be affected as I have already locked in a deal.

Individual Investor Menu
Dashboard
Change Password
My Portfolio
Analyze My Portfolio
Advance Analysis of Portfolio
Price List History
Daily Price List
Gainers
Unchanged
Losers
Sectors
Logout

FIG. 5: A SAMPLE CSCS ONLINE ACCOUNT MENU

Is the CSCS X-Alert any good?

In addition to using an online CSCS account, a good service that can help you keep track of transactions on your portfolio is one called CSCS X-Alert. The NSE introduced it for investors to receive notifications on their mobile phones via SMS when shares are traded on their stock accounts. The message will detail sales or purchases made and specify the volume, price and the stockbroker that executed the trade. If you didn't authorize the transaction, you can immediately abort the transaction by placing a call to CSCS/NSE. Trade alerts give you knowledge of inbound and outbound transactions on your account, thereby reducing chances of your account being defrauded or mismanaged.

Unfortunately, as things stand, investors aren't automatically enrolled for the service. To make matters worse, for all your transactions, you're automatically charged a flat fee for the service, whether you're enrolled or not. It's a pitiful process, you would say, but it's on you as the account holder to ensure that the alert service is set up on your account. The stock market is continually improving, so we can hope that at some point soon, the regulators will introduce automatic enrolment.

To get enrolled for the service, contact your stockbroker and request a CSCS X-Alert form. Complete and sign the form. Scan and return by email or in person. Your stockbroker will then submit the form to the CSCS for processing. If you prefer though, you can submit the form directly to the NSE/CSCS. The service is usually set up within forty-eight hours. You can also print out a copy of the form from the 'Download' section of the CSCS website. For those that already have the service activated, it's your responsibility to ensure that the phone number and email address details on your CSCS records are up to date.

The X-Alert service brings real-time notification, plus transparency, to the stock market whilst safeguarding investors against unauthorised transactions and improving their confidence. Get yourself set up. You can't go wrong.

X-Alert: CSCS-NSE
Trade 8/24/2020
11:00:00 AM;
DEAR JOE BLOGGS;
A/C:00012345 with
MERI; BUY NESTLE 280 units @ N
831.4000

FIG. 6: A SAMPLE OF NSE X-ALERT SENT VIA SMS

TIP NINE: Create Limit Orders

When buying or selling a stock, you may decide that you don't want to pay the market price. You have every power in your hands to choose to buy at a lower cost or sell at a higher price by placing a limit order rather than a market order. Although you get to specify the price, you may not get filled on your order if your limit price requirement isn't met. The market price will usually fluctuate throughout the trading day as investors buy and sell—it will rise if more people are buying and fall as more people sell.

Think of a market order as paying or being paid the market price when buying or selling a stock, meaning you will pay or receive whatever the current share price is. A market order is great if you need to get into a stock right away—if you're trading liquid stocks. A market order guarantees your order will be executed; however, it doesn't guarantee the execution price. The last-traded price isn't necessarily the price at which a market order will be executed.

A market price is the price of a stock on the open market at a given point in time as determined by the forces of demand and supply

Whether buying or selling, the online trading portal shows you a real-time stock quote to confirm the current price of the selected stock. Although you can view real-time stock prices, there is a limitation. As your web browser reloads, it fetches updated prices, but when you initiate a buy order, the price presented a few seconds ago may no longer be valid, as the market price may have changed. So since the prices of stocks are constantly fluctuating, the price of a stock at the time of execution may be slightly higher or lower than the last traded price. This dynamism can cause uncertainties in trades.

To counteract this problem, you can set a limit order for your trades. A 'buy' limit order will help you tell the stockbroker the maximum price you're willing to pay per share while a 'sell' limit order lets you designate the lowest price you are willing to accept.

Basically, with a limit order, you're instructing your broker that you don't want to buy or sell at the current price, but you want your order to be executed when the share price becomes more favourable. Although you can't haggle prices, you're free to specify what amount of money you're willing to spend at any given time.

A limit order is an order placed with a brokerage to buy or sell stock at a stipulated maximum purchase price or a minimum selling price

Limit orders will be of huge benefit to you if you can't monitor your stocks for some reason. You could be in bed sleeping or busy with other things and your limit orders would do your trading for you. When your limit price is reached, the trading system will automatically execute the order. Oftentimes, after being away from the trading platform, I come back to find money waiting from 'sell' orders automatically executed.

Personally, I hardly buy stocks at market prices, except if the purchase price of a stock I already own is much higher than its current market price. To get a good bargain, I set a limit price, especially if the stock price has been fluctuating massively in the last few days. Using the limit order feature allows me to gain better control of my orders.

For example, if Company Y stock has a market price of ₦ 10.00 and after checking the company fundamentals, I observe that the price had dropped to ₦9.50 at some point within the last few days, my instinct tells me that the current price of ₦10.00 may not be a good deal. What I am most likely to do in this case is to place a 'buy' limit order with a price limit of, say ₦9.55 or even ₦9.50. That limit price may be unrealistic for that day, so I would set an order term good for seven, ten or fourteen days during which the order will remain open.

When using the limit price option, you can only place a trade at a price within the price limit band for that particular day, otherwise, your order will be rejected.

DATE	ORDER TYPE	QUANTITY	SYMBOL	PRICE TYPE	TERM	ORDER STATUS	MARKET STATUS	MARKET MESSAGE	QUANTITY FILLED
4/6/2020	BUY	271.00	NESTLE	LIMIT @ 50.0	GOOD FOR THE DAY	CANCELLED	REJECTED	(295): Trade Rule - Price limit exceeded. Price cannot be less than 688.50	0

FIG. 7: A REJECTED ORDER SHOWING THE
PRICE LIMIT BAND FOR A TRADING DAY

If the system rejects my limit price, it will remind me of a major trade rule by specifying that the price limit entered has been exceeded. The stock trading platform is very intuitive, so it will display the minimum limit price possible for that trading period. If I think that the displayed limit price is justified—in line with my due diligence, I can go ahead and adjust my limit price to the one displayed, otherwise, I'll leave the trade for another day or just move on to the next stock on my wish list and repeat the process.

A limit order doesn't guarantee an execution. For example, if you set a limit order with an order term good for fourteen days, your order won't be executed if your limit price isn't reached within that period.

Instrument Type:
EQUITY

Symbol:
NESTLE NIGERIA PLC.

Order Type:
BUY

Quantity of Stock:
271.00

Price Type:
LIMIT

Price Limit:
765

Order Term:
GOOD FOR 14 DAYS

SUBMIT

FIG. 8: A SAMPLE LIMIT ORDER WORKFLOW

As previously mentioned, there are exceptional instances where I am happy to pay more than the market price. One of those instances is when the cost price for my portfolio stock is higher than its current market price. In this case, I may bump up my limit price to a price higher than the market price because my goal is to get filled at a price that will average down the purchase price of the stock.

Never rush into buying stocks at their current market prices. You need to find the right entry point. Do your due diligence and make use of the limit order functionality to buy at the best price for that period. Remember, the lower your purchase price, the higher the chances are of breaking even; and when share prices appreciate, the higher your capital gain.

I don't just sell a stock because the share price has appreciated. I usually set a limit order for a higher price if I believe I can get a bit more money, taking my personal profit margin rule into consideration; and of course, the recent trending prices. You can create limit orders for order terms depending on your requirements. I usually set up my limits to last for up to fourteen days, after which the order will expire if my price requirement doesn't hold true. My order term can be good for the day, good for seven days, ten days or fourteen days depending on the current behaviour of the stock.

With a limit order option, your order can be partially filled. For example, if you place a 'buy' limit order for 10,000 shares at a specified price for a seven-day order term and the price is met, but there are only 5,000 shares available for sale, the order will execute for partial shares and the limit order will remain open for the remaining unfilled shares until the expiration of the order term. The same applies to a 'sell' order. The whole process is automated, so you don't need to do anything.

One other benefit is that even when the market is closed, you can still place orders, however, the order can only be executed when the market reopens. A limit order good for one day will expire at the close of business for that day. If the order is good for multiple days, for example, seven days, it will close at the end of each business day and reopen automatically at the beginning of the next one until the end of the seventh day after which it will expire. You can manually cancel the order at any time.

One major drawback of a limit order is that if the stock is taking off with the price exploding and the growth moving to the upside, then you may miss out on your 'buy' trade and may need to adjust your limit price. For example, if your order hasn't been filled in your order term, then you may have to bump up your limit price until you get filled.

Whether you buy at a market or limit price will depend on your own personal goals. If you urgently need to get a stock, then paying the market price is totally fine if you don't care so much about the price sensitivity, but more about the time. If you care about the price and don't want to overpay, placing a limit order is in your best interest.

TIP TEN: Activate E-Dividend Mandate, Keep an Eye on Dividend and Bonus Declarations

Dividends generate a huge profit within the stock market, offering investors regular income and a hedge against share price fall. As already mentioned, dividends are issued to shareholders on a per-share basis. The more shares you own, the larger the dividend payment you receive. Dividend payouts allow you to benefit from earnings growth through interim and final dividends.

> A dividend is a portion of a company's earnings, paid to shareholders on a defined basis, for example, quarterly or annually

Why e-dividend?

Dividends are an indication that the underlying company is doing well. Basically, a company redistributes some of its earnings or profits to its shareholders in return for their investments. Not all companies pay dividends, but many financially stable companies do, and their dividend yield tends to grow over time. Historical dividend information is readily available if you care to know what has been paid out by different companies in the past. In fact, companies are becoming more transparent than ever before in the divulgence of financial information to investors.

Some companies make one dividend payment a year while some choose to split theirs, say twice a year. It doesn't really matter too much the number of times the dividend is paid in a financial year, it's just the way they split up the returns to shareholders. Cash dividends can also be paid when a company is liquidated and there is still some money to share after creditors have been paid off.

In recent years, concerted efforts have been made by the authorities to phase out dividend warrants (paper dividends) due to a myriad of issues associated with the issuance and posting of the warrants, including warrants getting lost in the post, investors not cashing out warrants within a six-month validity period, warrant revalidation, production costs, and so on.

The SEC, in its efforts to mitigate these issues, and as part of measures to curb the growth of unclaimed dividend and restore investors' confidence in the Nigerian stock market, the e-dividend scheme was brought into effect. All investors are required to register for the receipt of their dividends electronically—a process which has largely supplanted paper warrants and has the added benefit of ensuring that you never lose your dividends and are paid on time.

In simple terms, e-dividend allows investors to receive cash dividends through bank transfers. By registering for e-dividend, your registrars simply credit your bank account whenever dividend is paid by any of the companies you part-own.

E-dividend is the electronic transfer of dividends directly into a shareholder's nominated bank account, rather than the issuance of a paper warrant

You will only benefit from e-dividends if you've completed the e-dividend registration process. You'll have to set up an e-dividend mandate with all the registrars that keep the books of all companies you part-own. Sadly, registrars don't automatically set up e-dividend mandates for investors, even if they already have your bank details on record, so the onus is on you as the shareholder to ensure that you've an active e-mandate in place.

EDMMS saves the day

In the early years of the scheme, the e-dividend mandate enrolment was a very tedious process. Participation was painful—queuing up in banks to complete and sign the banker's confirmation form and travelling from one registrar's office to another to submit certified copies. To improve overall investors' experience, the SEC again reacted by launching the E-Dividend Mandate Management System (EDMMS) in collaboration with CBN and NIBSS. With the EDMMS, you can swimmingly set up an e-dividend mandate remotely, without visiting the banks or the registrars.

How does it work? The EDMMS portal utilizes a sophisticated document management system to which completed e-dividend mandate forms can be uploaded for central access. All you need to do is complete the e-dividend registration exercise by filling the e-dividend activation form and submitting it to the registrar. For those not physically present in Nigeria, you can send it by email. When the completed form is received, the registrar will verify details such as your name, account number and CHN. The form will then be uploaded to the EDMMS portal for immediate access by your nominated bank. The bank is required to validate your BVN and other account details.

If you choose to complete the e-dividend mandate form at your bank, the bank will upload a scanned copy of your completed form to the EDMMS portal. The uploaded form would immediately be accessible to the respective registrar. The portal serves as an online verification and communication medium for e-dividend mandate processing. It's a web-based application that can be assessed by every branch of all banks and by all registrars.

The following are the unique features or advantages of EDMMS:

I. Shareholders can go to their bank or any of its branches nationwide to complete an e-dividend mandate form and this will then be verified and stamped by the bank and forwarded electronically to the registrar.

II. Data relating to shareholders who are yet to provide their bank details to registrars have been pre-loaded onto the portal by NIBSS to allow the bank to verify shareholders' details online when they complete e-dividend activation forms.

III. Completed forms that have been verified by the bank will be forwarded electronically to the relevant registrar via the portal.

IV. Confirmation of forms and other correspondences between the registrar and the bank, as may be required, will be done via the portal.

V. Shareholders don't have to go to the registrar's office to submit e-dividend activation forms anymore.

If you're unsure whether your stock account has been mandated for e-dividend, you'll be able to check this information by contacting the respective registrar or using the U-eDiv Search tool on the SEC website (**Search online: sec nigeria u-ediv).** Once your stock is mandated, your dividends will be paid electronically to your bank account, including the previous ones you haven't yet received.

With the tremendous effort of introducing the e-dividend scheme by the authorities, a major problem still exists. As explained in **Tip Six: "Never Sell All the Shares of Your Stock"**, an e-dividend mandate isn't automatically set up for investors by registrars, even when you buy a stock administered by a registrar who already has your bank details on file. You must put some effort into ensuring that your stock account is mandated, for your own good.

If you've bought a new stock and a dividend is declared not long after, but you've not yet mandated the stock, how then do you get your dividend? One way is to ensure you've a postal address on record with all the registrars you deal with. When I say postal address, I mean a PO box address. The Nigerian postal system is inefficient. The days of effective postal delivery to physical or residential addresses are long gone. Delivery to PO box addresses is still possible, so the registrar may send a dividend warrant through this means. The warrant is usually valid for six months, giving you plenty of time to cash out. After six months, it will expire, but can be easily revalidated.

Getting a PO box is a lot easier now. You can complete an application online on the Nigerian Postal Service website (**search online: nipost nigeria post office box online**) and you'll be assigned a PO box after completion of the application process. You can track your application with a reference number and make payment at a preferred post office. For those that live abroad, there is no lifeline as you won't be able to receive dividend warrants. Get your stock accounts set up for e-dividend.

It's a good time to mention that the market regulators have gone beyond emphasising dividend payments alone. For selling-investors, there is now a direct cash settlement scheme in place that ensures a stockbroker can't sell without the investor's instructions. After the stockbroker sells your stock, rather than the proceeds going into the bank account of the stockbroker, it can now go directly to the investor.

Direct cash settlement of funds to your bank account isn't mandatory, but if you choose to have this option activated, you'll need to complete the direct cash settlement form (you can get a form from your stockbroker) and submit it to the stockbroker or registrar for processing.

I am not a big fan of the direct cash settlement option because I prefer the proceeds from my trades to go directly to the stockbroker who can instantly make a virtual credit to my stockbroking account. I can use the credit right away for new purchases. With the direct cash settlement option, I'll have to wait at least three working days for the trade to settle and the cash available. If there is a stock position I want to open quickly, I'll be unable to do as it will take even longer for the cash paid into my account to be transferred back to my stockbroking account. I don't like such delays.

Why invest in dividend stocks?

Dividend stocks provide the security of steady income that helps cushion investors' returns during industry downturns or market disruptions. At work, we are all excited and anxiously look forward to paydays—dividends give a similar feeling. Keeping an eye on dividend declaration is crucial to a healthy ROI. Knowing the exact dates that dividends will be paid gives a sense of fulfilment. Asset management institutions have made it simple for investors to remotely track the dates that profiting companies declare and pay dividends. But first, how do you really ensure that your stocks are dividend-prone?

The fundamental analysis of a dividend stock focuses on evaluating the ability of a company to grow its sales, profit margin, lower its debt and improve cash flow, out of which dividend is paid. Some companies pay dividends regularly while others seldom pay or don't pay at all. A pay-out is never guaranteed, but the chance of a pay-out is higher when the company's gross earnings, profit margin, and cash flow is growing significantly compared to previous financial years. This fundamental check is essential if you would like to invest in dividend-yielding stocks.

The dividend per share is a good index to determine a good dividend-yielding stock, but it's not all about that. An index significantly important is how the company has been paying out an incremental portion of its earnings to investors. Stocks with a consistent growth sequence in the last decade make good dividend-yielding stocks and will give peace of mind, at least.

I have a hankering for dividends. I prefer to invest in income stocks as they may require a lower level of ongoing capital investment, thus, profits can be directed back to me on a regular basis. Such stocks have for long been my golden goose. This doesn't mean I don't sometimes scout for penny stocks with strong fundamentals.

Using online tools and taking a look at my own dividend collection history, I have investigated companies that have consistently declared dividends in the last ten years or so—and the statistics have helped me in making key 'buy' decisions. I like the feeling of receiving dividends. Dividend-yielding stocks provide an extra income stream. Even when prices have fallen and there is no capital appreciation, dividend income provides some solace.

> Income or dividend stock is a stock that pays regular dividends and offers a high yield that may generate the majority of overall returns

These are some of the reasons you should consider dividend stocks:

I. Constant returns – Dividend stocks have a track record of generating a constant stream of income. With dividend-bearing stocks, you can be almost certain of earning a nice return. They're generally considered to be a lower risk investment due to the stability of the underlying companies. That's part of what makes dividend stocks a great way for long-term investors to get reliable returns, even in uncertain times.

II. Dividends are yours forever – When you earn a dividend, it remains yours even if you don't claim it immediately or in a number years to come. The only problem is that it may be eroded by inflation as the value reduces over the years. Unclaimed dividends are never owned by the companies who declare them and are separated from their assets.

III. Hedge against inflation – Dividend-bearing stocks with great yields can be a very good hedge against inflation. In an era where interest rates on savings are very low, earning dividends that pay yields higher than inflation basically guarantees a real positive return on your investment.

Bonus shares are also dividends as they do have a monetary value, albeit they are not cash payments. They're the company's accumulated earnings which aren't given out in the form of dividends but instead, are converted into free shares and issued to shareholders who can decide to sell the allotment in the stock market in exchange for cash.

Bonus share is an additional share issued to a shareholder at no extra cost, based upon the number of shares that the shareholder already owns at the time of the announcement of the bonus

The shares are paid from the reserves of the company and issued according to each shareholder's stake in the company. For example, if a company declares a bonus of 1 for 4, it means each shareholder will be entitled to one unit of share for every four held. So let's assume you've 10,000 shares of Company Y in your portfolio, a 1 for 4 bonus issue will see you get additional 2,500 shares for free. 'Every little helps'.

So how do I keep track of dividends and bonuses?

I. A good source of information is the NSE website
    (search online: nigeria nse dividends) where you
    can find, amongst other things, an updated list of
    companies that have declared dividends, the dividend
    per share, the date the dividend was announced,
    qualification date, closure of register, AGM date and
    payment date. I advise that you visit this website on a
    regular basis.

II. Besides the NSE, some agencies have online applications
    where dividend information can be tracked. One
    very popular one is Nairametrics **(search online:
    nairametrics dividends).** The website provides
    similar information to that of the NSE.

III. Some registrars have developed systems that trigger
    automated e-dividend payslips to investors. Once the
    registrar pays out a due dividend, you will automatically
    receive notification, so it's highly recommended that
    you have your email address registered with all the
    registrars you're involved with.

The e-bonus is here to stay—making the clumsiness of
gathering bonus share certificates for stock account reconciliation
a thing of the past. Similar to e-dividend, e-bonus transactions
are now more dynamic, making e-bonus the best way to get your
bonus entitlements. In this procedure, bonus issues are directly
credited to your CSCS stock account by the registrars. Your
stockbroker will also credit your stockbroking account accordingly.

E-bonus is the electronic transfer of bonus shares into
the CSCS system that contains the normal specific bonus
allocation for a given investor in place of a share certificate

When you log in to your CSCS online account you can view your earned bonuses. Based on your request, bonus shares are electronically detached and placed under the stockbroking firm of your choice. E-bonus eradicates the unnecessary time associated with the postage of certificates and eliminates theft or loss.

Company	DPS	Date Announced	Bonus	Closure of Register	AGM Date	Payment Date	Qualification Date
McNichols Consolidated Plc	N0.03k	1st April 2020	Nil	2nd - 8th July 2020	30th July 2020	7th August 2020	1st July 2020
NEM Insurance	N0.15k	1st April 2020	Nil	4th - 8th May 2020	to be announced	to be announced	30th April 2020
FCMB Group Plc	N0.14k	31st March 2020	Nil	15th – 17th April 2020	28th April 2020	28th April 2020	14th April 2020
Cadbury Nig. Plc	N0.49k	30th March 2020	Nil	25th - 29th May 2020	to be announced	to be announced	22nd May 2020
Beta Glass Nigeria plc	N1.67k	30th March 2020	Nil	15th - 19th June 2020	2nd July 2020	3rd July 2020	11th June 2020
Capital Hotel Plc	N0.05k	26th March 2020	Nil	20th - 24th April 2020	27th May 2020	3rd June 2020	17th April 2020
Sterling bank Plc	N0.03k	26th March 2020	Nil	5th - 8th May 2020	20th May 2020	20th May 2020	4th May 2020

FIG. 9: A SAMPLE OF DECLARED DIVIDENDS
WITH SCHEDULED PAYOUT DATES

Reclaim old dividends and check unclaimed dividend register

For investors that have acquired their stocks many years ago, but have never received any dividends, you'll need to put some effort into getting your unclaimed dividends. The first thing I advise you to do is request an updated list of all the stocks that you own in the CSCS by contacting your stockbroker. If you don't have a stockbroker, you will have to register with one to have access to the stock market, going forward. Read the section **'How to Open a Stockbroking Account'** for more detailed information on how to achieve this.

If you've any share certificates to hand, pass them over to the stockbroker.

The stockbroker will give you a share transfer form for the stocks you own. The purpose of the form is to mandate the stockbroker to act on your behalf and process your unpaid dividends.

Although the stockbroker will follow up with the registrars, it's a good idea for you to obtain a list of the respective registrars for the stocks you own. Every company has a registrar that manages its outstanding shares. The registrars are required to manage all shareholder issues, including dividends, share certificates, IPOs, bonus issues etc. So, it's important to know who your registrars are to know where your dividends are coming from.

If you've plenty of time on your hands and would rather follow up with the registrars yourself, you may decide to visit or contact all the registrars one after the other to enquire about your unpaid dividends. This may be a very time-consuming exercise, especially if your portfolio cuts across many registrars.

If you have accumulated unclaimed dividends for a stock which you have recently mandated for e-dividend, you would naturally expect the registrar to automatically pay the accumulated dividends into your nominated bank account as they now have your bank details on file. Sadly, this isn't usually the case. What happens in most cases is that the registrar only pays future dividends into your account, meaning the old dividends remain unpaid. If you've the old dividend warrants that are out of date, the best thing to do is to send scanned copies of the warrants directly to the registrar by email, asking that they be revalidated and paid into your designated bank account.

> An unclaimed dividend register is a book or publication that lists the names of investors that are yet to collect or claim the proceeds from their equities

There is a myriad of ways to check if you're registered for e-dividend or if you've unclaimed dividends. But why would anybody not want to collect the hard-earned profits from their investments and end up on the unclaimed dividend register? Sadly, there are several reasons why this happens. Some of these include:

I. Lack of information – Many investors are unaware that they have earned profits from their untracked investments, not to talk of claiming the profits.

II. Absence – Some investors have travelled abroad and believe nothing can be done until they return home.

III. Wrong address – Many investors have changed their addresses and as a result don't receive the dividend warrants sent to their previous addresses.

IV. Discouraging returns – Some investors with small portfolios believe dividend returns are too small to worry about or chase.

V. Forgotten investment, negligence

VI. Illness, death

As mentioned earlier, there's an electronic dividend search portal called U-eDiv Search that enables you to search whether you've dividends ready to be collected or if you've stock investments that are yet to be mandated for electronic payments. The only parameters required for the search are your first and last names. The search will return all the investors' names matching the search criteria and will display additional information like stock account numbers, company names and corresponding registrar names. You can easily identify yourself in the list by verifying that a displayed stock account number belongs to you. Every stock has a unique account number for every shareholder. Using this U-eDiv Search tool is the quickest and most convenient way to search for unclaimed dividends.

Annual reports are also good sources of information. Some companies publish in their annual reports, a list of shareholders that are yet to claim their dividends. You can lay a hand on a company's annual reports at the AGM or have it emailed to you by the registrar.

Another way to check is using registrars' portals. Some registrars have an updated register of unclaimed dividends on their website that you can search. If you find your name listed, contact the registrars without any delay and they will do the rest for you.

Some registrars have implemented Unstructured Supplementary Service Data (USSD) code that enables investors to make routine enquiries like dividend enquiry, shareholdings balance etc. on the go using their mobile phones. Your mobile number will have to be registered with the registrar in order to use this USSD code and a service charge may apply. Ask your registrar about the service.

A dividend left unclaimed gradually loses its value as investors don't earn interest on the unclaimed dividend, so for every day you delay to claim the reward on your investment, the value of your investment erodes. If the stock is worth investing in, the dividend is worth collecting.

TIP ELEVEN: Buy Your Stocks a Few Months Before Dividend Declaration or Right After a 'Guaranteed' Dividend

Optimism rally vs Pessimism rally

In the last two decennaries, the Nigerian stock market has consistently witnessed certain trends that industry professionals have termed optimism rally and pessimism rally. A rally is a period of sustained increases in stock prices. With the optimism rally trend, the stock market has consistently delivered positive returns mostly within the first half of the year. The pessimism rally trend has seen unfavourable returns delivered mostly within the second half of the year. Both trends suggest that in the Nigerian stock market, the chances of breaking even through capital appreciation by investing in the first half of the year is much higher than investing in the second half. Why are these trends happening and why have they been so consistent?

The reasons for these trends or their consistencies are not well defined but there are certain pointers. Generally, when a company beats its previous financial records, it's typically expected that the company increases or improves its dividend payout for the current fiscal year. Investors that know the market then anticipate a munificent return. As a result of this expectation or anticipation, smart investors will do their fundamental checks to analyse the stock before the company declares any dividend.

If the checks give positive signals, boom! This becomes the best time to acquire the stock or buy additional shares. The stock price is more likely to be lower at this time than after the dividend is declared. This is because, after the declaration, there would normally be a sudden rush by investors to acquire the underlying stock to qualify for dividend pay-out; as dividends are only paid to investors whose names appear in the register of shareholders by the closure date.

A Market rally describes a period of sustained increase in stock prices, especially after a period of flat or declining prices, caused by an increase in demand resulting from a heavy inflow of investment capital into the market

Most companies release their financial results in January, running up to March. A lot of dividend payments are made around April, May or June. Clearly, the first half of the year is a busy period. The second half of the year is a bit more laid back since most activities or actions take place in the first half. This workflow kind of justifies the claim of the industry professionals who have associated the first half of the year with optimism and the second half with pessimism.

So, how can you benefit from the optimism rally? The rally is a great opportunity for investors with a heavy focus on the appreciation of capital and also for those investing specifically in dividend stocks. Many stocks that offer attractive dividends above market average are found during this period, so missing them means having to wait until the following year.

If you acquire your stocks a couple of months before a dividend is declared (if any), this ensures that you'll buy at a lower price. The risk here, however, is that dividend isn't guaranteed, so there may not be a payout for the current fiscal year. I call it a risk for the sake of avoiding any argument or hullabaloo, but technically, it's no risk. If you've bought a stock at a good price, you'll laugh last in the long run, irrespective of any dividend declaration.

I personally like to save up funds running up to the end of the year to take advantage of the capital gains on stocks that have the potential to net dividends for the current financial year, but first, I audit selected stocks by checking price actions. Then, I review financial records to unveil the companies' balance sheets, revenue, profit, margin trends, trade volume etc. If I'm happy with the result, I go ahead and acquire as many shares as I can afford. With that ticked off, all that's left to do is wait for the anticipated dividends to be declared.

For investors who aren't comfortable doing due diligence, there is a lifeline. You can wait for the dividends to be declared before investing in the stocks. The caveat here is that you need to get the timing right. Once a dividend is declared, it's guaranteed to be paid and a pay date is scheduled, however, there would be an expected influx of investors attracted to the stock.

These investors want their own share of the company's profit, especially when they know that the dividend is guaranteed and they know exactly when it will be paid. Such an influx will inevitably lead to a higher demand for the stock and consequently, a higher share price as investors bid on the stock ahead of the payment date.

So, where does the timing factor come into play here? The price surge won't happen immediately after the dividend declaration. Share prices are governed by the forces of demand and supply, so it can take a couple of hours to a few days for the demand for that stock to get fully charged. If you time the market well and buy the stock right after the dividend is declared, you should be able to catch the stock at its crawling price.

If you do, then you can be almost certain that the price of the stock will be bumped up in no time. This strategy requires vigilance and availability of funds. You will have to ensure that your stock account is already funded and you're ready to pull the trigger. Some stockbrokers take a few days to credit investors' trading accounts with payments they receive via bank transfers, so the onus is on you to ensure you've cleared funds available.

Whether you buy your stock before dividend declaration or right after, there are two possibilities for financial reward. First, you can let the price rise to its limit for that period and cash out on capital appreciation, or you can leave it until the closure of register and qualify for dividend payment. Demand is expected to drop after the qualification date, and so is the price. Therefore, if you like to liquidate your holdings after this period, you may have to wait long to do so.

A lot of corporate actions are released to the investing public between February and May, with the dividend qualification date mostly falling within the same period. For long-term investors that are more focused on income or growth stocks, there can't be a better option than ensuring you acquire your stocks early before the qualification date in order to qualify for dividends. We shall discuss this later in **Tip Twelve: "Check Qualification Date Before You Buy or Sell"**. As an Investor, especially one who buys and holds dividend-paying stocks, be wise to understand how dividends work.

TIP TWELVE: Check Qualification Date Before You Buy or Sell

If you've missed out on buying stocks a few months before dividend declaration or right after a dividend was declared, it's not all doom and gloom. Investors that are ardent traders of income stocks may still consider buying shares before the dividend qualification date. When companies declare or announce dividends, they append a date when the register of shareholders will close—only shareholders who own shares listed in their register by the qualification date will be paid dividends.

The qualification date (or ex-dividend date) is a very important one. All shareholders who are on the company's books as at the close of business on the qualification date are entitled to receive dividends. The qualification date is usually the last working day before the company starts to compile a register of its shareholders. It can take anything up to one week for the company to compile the register, but unfortunately, if you don't own your shares by the qualification date, your name won't appear in the register.

> Qualification date is the cut-off date by which a company's shares must be owned for the investor to be eligible for dividend payment for the current financial year

It's good practice to check if the stock you're buying can earn you dividends. Of course, you can make money by selling for a capital gain, but how about profiting twice—getting a dividend and then later selling the shares at a higher price? It's a win-win, right? So, before you place that order, one of the things you may benefit from is to check whether the company has recently declared a dividend. If the company has made a recent dividend announcement, the qualification date would have been scheduled. As discussed, you'll get a dividend pay-out on the pay date if you own the stock before the qualification date.

Pay attention to the word 'own'. It's different from 'buy'. The caveat is that there is a T+3 rule (transaction day plus three working days) in place, so, if you buy your stock today, it will take three working days for the trade to settle and for the shares to be credited to your CSCS account. To qualify for the dividend, the shares must be bought at least three working days before the qualification date. If you buy on the qualification date, you'll not get the dividend, rather, the seller of the stock will get it because they own the stock as at that date.

Although the dividend is guaranteed, it's never a full ROI. It's usually a small percentage of your capital, but it's still a profit, regardless. The dividend is said to be guaranteed because it's based on the profit that the company earned in the previous financial year or quarter, not on a projected profit.

To sell the stock, you don't need to wait until the pay-out date. You can sell before then and still get the dividend, as long as you keep the stock until the qualification date. If the share price falls after the qualification date, you must wait until the stock rebounds, to realise a capital gain. This strategy is called the dividend capture strategy. It's a simple, no-nonsense, income-focused strategy that requires no financial or technical stock analysis. The strategy works best when an investor has a long-term trading approach as it may take some time for fallen prices to rise again.

I have developed a habit of checking the dividend calendar regularly. These days, my purchases are mostly inspired by the calendar. In fact, my 'buy' workflow starts by checking it. I do due diligence on financially stable companies that have declared dividends. If I'm happy with the fundamentals, I consider buying the stock. This doesn't necessarily mean that if a company hasn't declared a dividend, I wouldn't consider buying its shares. If I anticipate a dividend, I would strongly consider investing. Each stock is different, so it all depends on each stock's situation.

> Dividend capture strategy is an investment strategy involving the timed purchase and subsequent sale of dividend-paying stocks, executed by buying a stock just before the qualification date, in order to receive the dividend, then selling it immediately after the dividend is paid

So, how do you keep tabs on dividend qualification dates? It's super easy. Visit the NSE website (**search online: 'nse nigeria closure of register'**).

There you'll find a table that displays the dividend per share declared for various stocks for the current and previous financial years. You can view closure of register, AGM, and payment dates. The webpage is regularly updated as new companies declare dividends. The site is the official source of dividend information for the Nigerian stock market.

Another reliable source of information is the Nairametrics web application (**search online: nairametrics qualification date**). Similar to the NSE website, this webpage also specifies closure of register dates for all companies that have declared dividends. In addition, it specifies the qualification dates.

Both capital gain and dividend are a healthy source of income, but for me, capital gain takes priority. If a stock has appreciated in value by a decent margin, I won't hold it back just to earn a dividend. I will normally sell for capital gain. The reason is simple, the earnings I realise from a capital gain in one financial period is much more than that from a dividend for the same period.

Still, it's a regular practice for me to check if a stock is near its qualification date before I attempt to sell it. If the qualification date is near and I see the potential of the stock still netting a capital again in the near future, I can hold on to the stock for capital gain and dividend. If the qualification date is far ahead, I will cash out. If you've owned a stock for months or years and you sell it before the next qualification date, you won't get the dividend for the current period, irrespective of how long you have kept the stock. When it comes to investing, knowing your dates is important.

TIP THIRTEEN: Attend Annual General Meetings Whenever Possible

At the end of every financial year, most companies file their financial results and organise an AGM between shareholders and the directors. The meeting is an opportunity for the company management to present a perspicuous annual report containing some essential information to stakeholders about the company's performance, helping to ensure transparency.

An annual general meeting is a meeting of the general membership of an organisation, where the organisation discusses its business activities and presents its audited annual report and accounts to shareholders

The meeting plays a unique role in the journey of an equity investor. It will arm you with the information you need to make critical investment decisions. At the meeting, you'll be presented with a rare opportunity to meet the company's directors who share company insights with their shareholders about the last financial year's business performance, strategies, and the position of the business vis-a-vis the incoming financial year. Investors question the board, get answers for unsatisfactory performance, and challenge the management on the direction of the company.

The registrar will send, for your review, an electronic copy of the annual report by email, usually as a file that can be downloaded on your device or printed as a book. This practice is in line with SEC's directive and to ensure that the report gets to shareholders before the meeting. It's important that you've your email address in the books of the registrars. The registrar will send you a notification by email to inform you of the forthcoming AGM—date, time and venue. Annual reports contain some vital information about the health of the company in which you've invested. The better you're at understanding a company's annual report, market conditions and growth trajectory; the better the stock trader you'll become.

> An annual report is a yearly audited record that details a company's performance, operations, financial position and corporate activities

Getting accredited for an AGM has been largely simplified within the Nigerian stock market. Gone are the days when investors had to wait for invitation cards to arrive through the post. Many were unable to attend as the cards never arrived or arrived late. Accreditation in the old days was solely done in person at the meeting venues. The chaos caused at venues led to many investors boycotting the meetings altogether.

Digitisation has brought succour to the notification and accreditation processes. Online pre-registration for attendance at the annual general meeting is now available and can be achieved by accessing the "E-accreditation" link that is included in the meeting circulars sent to all investors via email. E-accreditation only applies to shareholders who have provided their phone number, email address, bank account number or BVN to the registrars.

Once a dividend is declared through a corporate action, it's subjected to shareholders' ratification or approval at the AGM before it's eventually paid. All companies offering dividends must wait till the AGM date, at the earliest, to make the payments.

AGM creates the opportunity to question, correct, or advise the management on the modus operandi of the company. It also bestows the opportunity to network with fellow shareholders and to vote on current issues—company's board of directors, executive compensation, dividend payments and so on.

The meeting puts a perfect opportunity on your lap to review the company's audited financial statements comprehensively, question any irregularities observed, and seek clarifications. All the things you hear and the signs you see at the meeting can help you re-evaluate your part-ownership and decide what your next move is. Are the signs positive? Is the company in the right direction? Are the directors committed to business growth? Are the newly announced business models promising? You decide.

It may not always be possible to attend AGMs, especially for those that live abroad or even outside of the venue city. These days, many companies have been holding live AGMs online. Investors are emailed the video link to join the AGM. So, irrespective of your location, you can participate.

TIP FOURTEEN:
Consider Buying Rights

When a company wants to raise additional capital to expand its business, it may turn to a bank for an interest-yielding loan or it could do a rights issue by approaching its shareholders for more money, giving them the entitlement to purchase new shares at a predetermined price (normally less than the current market price), in proportion to the number of shares already owned. Because the discounted shares appear attractive, shareholders buy the shares and the company, as a result, gets the money it needs for the proposed expansion of the business. So, it's a win-win situation for both parties.

> A right issue is an offer to shareholders of an organisation to purchase additional shares not offered to the public, usually at a price below the market price

The whole process starts with a company submitting an application to the NSE for approval and listing a rights issue of a certain number of ordinary shares at a certain price based on a specified allocation ratio, for example, one new ordinary share for every two ordinary shares held (1 for 2).

After approval, the registrar will send a copy of rights circular to all shareholders, informing them of the rights offer, not less than twenty-one days before the opening of the rights issue. The circular will detail the number of shares currently held, number of rights due, amount payable and the closing or record date. If you've an email address on the coffers of the registrar, you'll get this notification by email with an application form that can be downloaded and printed. The quickest way to join the wagon is to complete the form, sign and return it by email to the registrar or your broker with the consideration value of the rights plus any regulatory fees.

After the closing date, your shares shall be allotted to you after confirmation that the right's consideration has been fully paid. Your allotted shares will be sent by the registrar to the CSCS, who in turn credits your CSCS account with the new shares. It may take a few weeks for your online CSCS and stockbroking accounts to be updated.

The additional shares you acquire average down your total cost price for that stock; theoretically, you get more shares at a discount and have a bigger portfolio, so if the market price of the stock increases, you gain more. A rights issue enables you to maintain your proportionate stake in the company.

For a clear understanding, let's look at a rights issue scenario. You own 1,000 shares in Company Y and each share is trading at ₦50.00. The company intends to fund some acquisitions and growth strategies and needs to raise cash. Therefore, it announces a rights issue, in which it plans to raise ₦30 million by issuing 10 million ordinary shares to existing shareholders at a price of ₦30.00 each. Assuming that this rights issue is 2 for 10, in other words, for every 10 shares held, Company Y is offering you 2 shares at a discounted price of ₦30.00 per share. Since you hold 1,000 shares, you are entitled to buy 200 additional shares during the rights issue at the discounted price of ₦30.00 per share. This price is 40% less than the ₦50.00 price at which the company's shares currently trades. The difference between the offer price of the rights and the market price of the shares represents the rights premium.

What can I do with the offer?

You don't necessarily have to accept the offer. Rights have a value and can be traded. You can either renounce or trade the entirety to shareholders or other interested investors, or partially accept it by buying only a fraction. For example, if you're due 200 rights, you can buy 100 and trade the rest. The trading of the rights compensates investors for any future dilution of their current holdings in the company.

During the subscription period of a rights issue, several options are available to you.

I.   You can take up the rights issue in full, and pay the relevant rights price to the Issuer.

II.   Trade the entirety of the rights to existing shareholders or other interested investors.

III.   You can take up part of the rights and trade the rest.

IV.   You can ignore the rights offer, do nothing, and let the rights expire.

Of course, it's a forward-moving idea to know the purpose of the additional funding or understand what the company intends to use the money for before accepting or rejecting a rights issue. Luckily, because of the kind of regulatory issues that supervise the stock market, the company would publish a circular which would explain what the money from the proposed rights issue is meant for. Not only that, the regulatory authorities then track whether the company has utilised those funds as intended. This way, investors can be sure that the money is going to be used on that basis. If you are convinced, then you should consider subscribing to the rights issue.

A rights issue isn't often offered by a company, so when there is an offer available, consider accepting it, but of course, as usual, take the company's performance and fundamentals into consideration. The underlying analytical issues that you need to look at when buying shares on a rights issue remain the same as when you are buying shares at market price, so if a company is doing well and has a good expected return, then you should be happy as a lark to improve your stake in the company at a discounted price.

TIP FIFTEEN: Reinvest Your Gains and Diversify Your Portfolio

A stock portfolio is a very liquid investment, as converting it into cash only takes a transaction. Within a few seconds or minutes, the transaction could be done and dusted with the investor smiling to the bank. To cash out on shares, all you need to do is place a 'sell' order from your online trading platform. If there is a buyer on the other side, the transaction happens in a twinkle of an eye. No paperwork is needed and no chain of intermediaries is involved. After the settlement date (transaction plus three working days), the cash will be available to you.

It can be rewarding to reinvest your capital gains or dividends. With the high liquidity level of stocks, it's advised that profits from capital gains and dividends are reinvested into stocks. The benefits can pay off as time flies by.

Capital gain reinvestment is the buying of new or additional shares with the profit from a stock sale, rather than take cash

Reinvest the gains

Dividend reinvestment is an investment strategy that brings sustainable wealth and helps to raise investment income as time goes by. It's one of the cheapest ways possible to multiply your small investment until it grows into a lifetime portfolio. Dividend stocks offer a radically consistent increase in dividend payout. You get an increase in the shares you own and improve your returns and the value of your portfolio over time. With the inevitable upward and downward movement of stock prices, dividend reinvestment provides the leverage that grows your returns aggressively. Small dividends can add up to powerful gains if they are invested regularly.

Dividend reinvestment is the buying of new or additional shares with the profit from a dividend, rather than take cash

The greatest power in finance is compound interest. If you're to reinvest all the dividends you receive from dividend-bearing stocks, it will compound the overall value of your portfolio as you earn dividends on the dividends you receive. So while investing in dividend-bearing securities can be a good way to generate regular investment income, reinvesting the funds in stocks will greatly increase your ROI.

For a clear understanding, let's look at a scenario of how dividend reinvestment can increase returns when investing in stocks that have strong fundamentals. Assuming Company Y has an enviable dividend payment history, having been consistent with dividend payments to shareholders in the last five years, declared ₦1.00 dividend per share two years ago and the stock traded at ₦20.00 the same day. So, an investor that owns 50,000 shares would net ₦50,000 dividend. Assuming that the money is reinvested that day, the owner would bag an additional 2,500 shares, raising their total holdings to 52,500 shares.

The company declared ₦1.80 dividend per share last year and traded at ₦27.50, meaning that the investor would rake in ₦94,500 in dividend payment. Reinvesting the cash that same day yields 3436 additional shares, taking the investor's holding to 55,936 shares.

Going forward, the company declared ₦2.60 dividend per share this year and traded at ₦35.40. This ensures a dividend return of ₦145,434. Reinvesting this sum boosts the investor's holdings by 4108 shares to 60,044 shares. This scenario assumes all things being equal with an annual rise in dividend per share. For many blue-chip companies, this scenario is a common occurrence.

Diversification is key to maintaining a well-balanced portfolio

Portfolio diversification is an essential stock trading strategy which involves spreading your money across a variety of securities, so you aren't exposed to one risk. Strategies like diversification and appropriate asset allocation can help beat inflation over the long-term.

Stock diversification is a process of owning different stocks that tend to perform well at different times in order to reduce the effects of volatility in a portfolio and also increase the potential for increasing returns

Diversification is made up of two major concepts— diversification by sector and by size. The sectors are the different areas of the market while the size is the amount of money being invested. The whole idea of stock diversification is that you don't want to put all your money into one sector of the market, rather you want to spread your money by buying stock positions across multiple sectors of the economy, making your portfolio a lot safer.

When you diversify across sectors, you're not only diversifying your risk and returns, you could also benefit from dividend payment, especially if your portfolio contains a ragbag of sectors (mostly financial services, agriculture, consumer goods etc.) that are known for paying dividends.

In the haste to make it big in the market, investors are often tempted to invest all their money in the stock market all at once. While this may be profitable, it may also work to your disadvantage. There's a greater tendency to reduce risk and increase returns if you slowly but regularly build your stock portfolio with periodic investments and diversification over time.

The importance of a well-diversified stock portfolio in any market condition can't be overemphasized. The stock acquisition is great but putting all of your money in one stock or sector of the market can be risky. Instead of purchasing one stock, purchase a variety. This reduces the risk that one or more companies will fail and wipe out a large portion of your portfolio. As you add more securities to your portfolio, you reduce specific company and industry risks. Eventually, you'll only be exposed to systematic risks—the risks inherent in an entire stock market. Portfolio diversification is an important safeguard if any one type of stock or industry fails or underperforms.

There are different diversification methods that you can incorporate into your portfolio:

I.   Include multiple securities – Not just investing in one or two stocks that you know and/or think will do really well but adding some others to reduce the risk that if one stock does poorly, your whole portfolio will too. Companies can go to zero, markets don't.

II.   Diversify across major asset classes – Depending on your goals and risk tolerance, include stocks that have different reactions to the changing economy and reduce the volatility of your portfolio.

III. Diversify across sectors – You're not fully diversifying if you're only investing in stocks within the same industry sector. They usually have a similar reaction to the economy. Exposure to different sectors will have different reactions to market conditions like rising interest rates, for example. If market conditions change, your portfolio won't all decline at the same time.

Investing in many different stocks will help build your wealth by leveraging growth in different sectors of the economy, resulting in a profit even if some lose value.

Currently, at the NSE, there are twelve industry sectors under which companies can be listed. These include:

- Agriculture
- Conglomerates
- Construction/ Real Estate
- Consumer Goods
- Financial Services
- Healthcare
- Industrial Goods
- Information and Telecommunications Technology
- Natural Resources
- Oil and Gas
- Services
- Utilities

Diversifying across sectors should be done wisely. I'm incredibly finicky about the sectors I put my money in, so I mostly research and invest in ones whose stocks offer high liquidity. Liquidity drives price and makes the buying and selling of shares much faster. I consider buying shares that are heavily traded daily. This makes life easier to find buyers when it's time to cash out and also helps me take advantage of high-volume transactions that can drive prices higher in a bullish market.

By spreading your investments across several sectors, you've a better chance of participating in the growth of some of your stocks at any one time. A portfolio with the same expected return, but with lower volatility will outperform. It allows you to rebalance your portfolio and reduces your desire to bail out of your portfolio because you can't handle the huge losses.

Diversification is usually called the only free lunch in investing and this is so because you reduce the risk within your portfolio by adding more non-correlated securities without reducing your expected return. However, while you don't give up the expected return, you do give up something, which is the chance that your next big stock will hit it out of the park. With broad diversification, you'll still be holding those winners, but they will be a small proportion of your portfolio and won't make you an instant millionaire.

With all said, the whole point of portfolio diversification is that you're managing risk. You're hedging risk because if one sector is doing really well, you will be making money, but if another sector isn't, its value may go down, and that's why you shouldn't keep everything in one sector. Diversification is very important especially when you are investing for the long-term. It's all about the sector and size.

The key is to spread your money around in a size proportionate way across different sectors. That's what you are trying to accomplish when you diversify your portfolio. A diversified portfolio provides the potential to improve ROI. As your investment grows, consider owning a mix of stocks. Diversification is important in terms of ROI and peace of mind.

TIP SIXTEEN: Trade As a Long-term Investor But Capitalise on Short-term Opportunities

There is more than one way to approach the stock market and many different schools of thought exist on how best to make money trading stocks. The equities market is long-term in nature, so the most common trading strategy is to buy and hold unto an investment—for many years. This has for long been the most conventional approach, but not always the wisest.

In Nigeria, it's common to find investors who use equity investment as a retirement plan, which means their acquired equities will not be sold until they retire or are no longer able to work. As reasonable as that sounds, it's a parochial approach to wealth creation. Is there something wrong with cashing out on a stock that has appreciated in value and reinvesting the funds in the same stock or portfolio? Certainly not!

There's usually more money to be made investing in the long run than chasing yields in the short-term, however, market deviations occur rather too frequently in the short-term that provides daring investors ample opportunities to make decent profits.

Is it advisable to have a long-term trading approach?

Yes, due to portfolio losses associated with short-term stock volatility in the stock market, it's advisable to have a long-term outlook when buying stocks, if you're seeking to make good money or gain discernible results from equity investment. In fact, as a simple rule, when buying stocks, you shouldn't use money that you need in the short-term. Invest with the long-term in mind. You're very likely to make good returns if you invest in stocks that have strong fundamentals and maintain a long-term prospect. Long-term investing allows you to manage your risk by evaluating the companies you're investing in, finding an edge, buying them at the right price, and being very confident that, over time, they're going to increase in value and make you money.

A long-term investor is one with the intention of holding onto an investment for a long period of time (usually years) by looking past the day-to-day fluctuations of the stock market

A long-term investor is usually willing to accept a certain quantum of risk in pursuit of potentially higher rewards and possess the attribute of being able to be patient for a longer period. Basically, you want to buy into a business you're willing to be part of for the long-term because the daily ups and downs of the stock market are extenuated by the long-term effect where the share prices will over time go up.

Many long-term investors invest in growth stocks with the hope that the companies reinvest their profits. Currently in Nigeria, a company with a five-year average dividend payout less than 30% of earnings is classified as a growth stock.

> A growth stock is a stock which typically doesn't pay a
> dividend, as the company declares its choice to reinvest
> earnings in capital projects

If you're looking into which long-term stocks to buy and hold, I would say find the ones which are consistent and pay the highest dividends. While waiting for your investment to beat inflation in the coming years, the dividends will keep you happy. In addition, long-term trading is easier, less expensive tax-wise and less risky when compared to short-term trading.

> A short-term investor is one with the intention of owning an
> investment only for a relatively short period of time (usually
> for days, weeks or a couple of months) and monitoring the
> day-to-day fluctuations of the stock market with the ambition
> to sell the investment when the market price increases or
> becomes favourable

To mitigate long-term investing risks, you should consider owning stocks that have proven records of delivering strong profitability growth and have a great competitive edge over their competitors. This provides you with a margin of safety or a hedge for your long-term portfolio and gives you the grounds to enjoy the benefits of dividend investing.

Although you're buying stocks with a long-term outlook, you should keep your eyes peeled and constantly track the progress of your portfolio, so that if an attractive opportunity arises, you are ready to sell. You need to constantly garner information that can help you make key 'sell' decisions. This is where short-term trading comes in.

Investing in the short-term

Short-term investments have the advantage of growth potential in a short period of time. I ask again: Is something wrong with cashing out on a stock that has appreciated in value and reinvesting the funds in the same portfolio? It's unclear why many long-term investors fail to see the prospects of capitalising on quick short-term gains. I like to lock in profits by selling any investment that has appreciated in value considerably. Afterwards, I wait for the stock price to fall again or better still, find another stock in the oversold region, but with the potential for a price bounce. This way, I can compound the overall value of my portfolio.

Short-term investors use a strategy that relies heavily on timing the market, taking advantage of short-term events to rake in a profit within a short period of time (minutes, hours, days, weeks or months). Timing the stock market is never an easy task, but gains can sometimes be realised in a day or so. This is especially true when the market is exuberant and stocks are rallying upwards—a bullish period.

There may be a lot of different reasons why an investor may close out a stock trade or a position earlier than anticipated. They include the following:

I.   To take profits off the table – If a stock has already run up a huge amount compared to what it normally does, an investor may close that trade after looking at a projective move of their A to B, B to C and C to D patterns, so it's already hitting its move and the risk to reward ratio may not be there. In this case, they take the profit off the table by closing the trade because the risk to reward ratio is no longer in their favour.

II.   When prices swing up and down considerably – When a stock swings all over the place haphazardly in price and become very volatile, for example, a new IPO and investors don't have a clear view or vision of direction, so with the extra added volatility, they don't like trading such stocks as they don't offer clean charts.

III. When a stock isn't behaving properly – An investor may sell a stock if it's not behaving as projected, not retracing with the expected volume or if they are having doubts. There could be a change in shift or momentum or a change in people's mindset about the stock, so things may not always be in their favour.

Generally, you want to find and trade stocks that will end up in your favour because that is when you will have a high probability of success. For me, I don't sell a stock unless it's for a realised profit, otherwise, I am happy to hold on for as long as possible. Even though I buy stocks with a view of holding a long-term portfolio, I scavenge for short-term opportunities by consistently tracking price movements. If I find a favourable upward movement in stock price with a decent ROI, I will cash out. Why not?

Cashing out doesn't end my interest in the stock, it only means I have increased my buying power by acquiring a larger stake because I now have the funds to do so. After selling, I have two options: One, I can wait for the price of the same stock to drop below my selling price, so I can buy again, or two, I can reinvest the capital plus profit in new stock. Whichever way, I would still have a portfolio. This is a short-term trading approach, but a long-term portfolio.

Long-term or short-term investment, which is better?

I trade as both a short-term and a long-term investor. My stock position determines my attitude towards my investment or whether I should keep a stock in the long-term or trade it in the short-term. Whenever possible, I do day trading, which is when one buys a stock then sells for gain on the same day. Day traders move in and out of trades and capitalise on price fluctuations. There are situations where stock appreciates minutes or hours after purchase. I have made some ridiculous profit using this no-nonsense approach.

For short-term investors (except for those actively practising the dividend capture strategy), dividend payout isn't an important factor in their decision-making as all they are after is cashing out on the value created when the share prices increase. Capital gain is their main focus and the ultimate goal.

Whether long or short-term trading, each strategy has its strengths and weaknesses. You can make some lightning-quick returns from day trading, which is a short-term strategy, but it can be pricey since you're trading frequently. It can also make you become greedy with acquisitive goals which often results in taking higher risks. The goal is to take advantage of small fluctuations in price leveraged over large investments in order to make a profit.

For example, if a stock fluctuates by ₦1.00 in a given day, for a long-term investor, this temporary increase is almost meaningless, however, if a short time trader was to buy 100,000 shares and sell at the new market price, they make ₦100,000 for the day on that stock. This type of short-term profit is alluring, but it's difficult to gain higher returns than the average rate of the stock market. Also, tracking price fluctuations requires a lot of time and dedication with constant monitoring of one's investments.

On the other hand, long-term investment is more time-efficient as you don't require much time to monitor your investments or price fluctuations, it's cheaper to practise, helps to achieve portfolio diversification, and it's generally easier to navigate the stock market in a bearish period. However, you need to be patient to realise robust gains through annual returns or compounding.

When it comes to investing, it's important to find the right approach for you and your individual situation. Before you start investing, be it short or long-term, you should have clear goals in mind. One thing is certain—approaching the stock market with a long-term focus but capitalising on short-term opportunities can create sustainable wealth.

USEFUL ONLINE RESOURCES

For this book to live up to its goal of being a resource, this section has been garnished with URLs of various web pages and online resources. The web is a powerhouse of information, however, knowing where to find the relevant information and using the right search words can save you ample time and enrich your browsing experience.

I must stress at this juncture that the shared web addresses and online resources are available and valid at the time of writing. By the time you are reading this, some of the resources may be obsolete, for different reasons, including links being renamed, moved, blocked, or deleted. Across the web, the content, design, and infrastructure of many websites evolve quite frequently and, as a result, the location of materials or records are bound to change. If for any reason, you can't access any of the listed sites or links, not to worry, you will be able to search online using certain keywords appended beneath the URLs that can quickly lead you to the relevant information.

The whole essence of sharing the online resources here is to sensitise you to the fact that there are applications or tools out there that can help you achieve the most from stock trading and managing your portfolio effectively. You get the idea.

Registrars' and stockbrokers' websites are always a vital source of information. The easiest and quickest way for investors to find information about their investments is to visit the website of the underlying registrar or that of the stockbroker. The registrars' websites usually have a dedicated client information section that gives detailed corporate information about their individual client, including dividend and bonus history, company reports, unclaimed dividend, AGM, corporate actions and so on.

Below, you'll find a list of all registrars currently trading in Nigeria with their web addresses and search keywords to help find them online in the event of a changed web address. Once you're on the website, navigate to the section dedicated to clients. The section is usually titled like 'Client Information', 'Our Clients', 'Clients' 'Client Portfolio' etc.

Some stockbrokers have consistently performed in the last few years and have built up trust and reputation amongst investors and regulatory bodies. Their performances are measured using the volume and value of trade indices. A compiled list of stockbrokers that fall into this category can be found below.

Also listed are useful websites and keywords that can help you find all sorts of key information online. These include platforms where you can keep track of daily stock prices, get general information about the Nigerian stock market, find a licenced stockbroker, check listed companies, set up a CSCS online account, check unclaimed dividend register, analyse stock performance, check dividend declarations, find mutual fund managers etc. Online possibilities are endless.

NSE Nigeria:
Website: http://www.nse.com.ng
Search online: nse nigeria

Check dividend declarations and payout dates:
Website: http://www.nse.com.ng/Listings-site/corporate-disclosure-site/Pages/Closure-of-Register.aspx
Search online: nse nigeria dividends

Website: https://nairametrics.com
Search online: nairametrics dividends

Check the directory of licenced stockbrokers:
Website: http://www.nse.com.ng/dealing-members/find-a-dealing-member/dealing-member-directory
Search online: nse nigeria dealing members directory

CSCS Nigeria:
Website: https://www.cscs.ng
Search online: cscs nigeria

CSCS Nigeria online account registration:
Website: https://portal.cscs.ng/home/register
Search online: cscs nigeria registration

Check daily share price:
Website: http://www.nse.com.ng/market-data/trading-statistics
Search online: nse nigeria daily price list

Website: https://www.cscs.ng/market-information/daily-price
Search online: cscs nigeria daily price list

Website: https://www.stanbicibtcstockbrokers.com/research/pricelist?Equities
Search online: stanbic ibtc equities price list

Check the database of unregistered investors for e-dividend:
Website: https://sec.gov.ng/non-mandated
Search online: sec nigeria u-ediv

Check the companies listed on the NSE:
Website: http://www.nse.com.ng/issuers/listed-securities/listed-companies
Search online: nse nigeria listed companies

Check the industry sectors under which companies can be listed at the NSE:
Website: http://www.nse.com.ng/issuers/listing-your-company/industry-sector
Search online: nse nigeria industry sectors

Check weekly market reports:
Website: http://www.nse.com.ng/market-data/other-market-information/weekly-report
Search online: nse nigeria weekly report

Analyse stock performance:
Website: https://www.easykobo.com/Home
Search online: easykobo nigeria

Website: https://www.bloomberg.com
Search online: investing equities performance

Website: https://www.investing.com/equities/nigeria
Search online: bloomberg equities performance

Stock comparison platform:
Website: https://www.easykobo.com/CompareStocks
Search online: easykobo nigeria stock comparison

Check the validity of BVN:
Website: https://nibss-plc.com.ng/bvn
Search online: nibss nigeria bvn

List of company registrars in Nigeria:

Africa Prudential PLC
Website: https://africaprudential.com
Search online: africa prudential registrars nigeria

All Crown Registrars Limited
Website: http://www.allcrownregistrarsltd.com
Search online: all crown registrars nigeria

Apel Capital Registrars Limited
Website: http://registrars.apel.com.ng
Search online: apel registrars nigeria

Atlas Registrars Limited
Website: https://atlasregistrars.com
Search online: atlas registrars nigeria

Cardinalstone Registrars Limited
Website: https://cardinalstoneregistrars.com
Search online: cardinalstone registrars nigeria

Carnation Registrars Limited
Website: https://carnationregistrars.com/
Search online: carnation registrars nigeria

Centurion Registrars Limited
Website: http://centurionregistrars.com
Search online: centurion registrars nigeria

DataMax Registrars Limited
Website: https://datamaxgroup.ng
Search online: datamax registrars nigeria

EDC Registrars Limited
Website: https://www.edcregistrars.com.ng
Search online: edc registrars nigeria

First Registrars Nigeria Limited
Website: http://www.firstregistrarsnigeria.com
Search online: first registrars nigeria

GTL Registrars & Data Solutions Limited
Website: https://www.gtlregistrars.com
Search online: gtl registrars nigeria

Lighthouse Registrars Limited
Website: http://registrars.lighthouse.com.ng
Search online: lighthouse registrars nigeria

Meristem Registrars Securities Limited
Website: https://www.meristemng.com
Search online: meristem registrars nigeria

PAC Registrars Limited
Website: http://www.pacregistrars.com
Search online: pac registrars nigeria

Sterling Registrars Limited
Website: http://www.sterlingregistrar.com
Search online: sterling registrars nigeria

United Securities Limited
Website: https://www.unitedsecuritieslimited.com
Search online: united securities nigeria

Unity Registrars Limited
Website: https://unityregistrarsng.com
Search online: unity registrars nigeria

Veritas Registrars
Website: http://www.veritasregistrars.com
Search online: veritas registrars nigeria

Check weekly top ten broker performance:
Website: http://www.nse.com.ng/dealing-members/
member-performance
Search online: nse nigeria broker performance

21 stockbrokers that have consistently performed within the last few years. This is listed in alphabetical order with no positions assigned:
ARM Securities Limited
Website: https://armsecurities.com.ng
Search online: arm securities nigeria

Apel Asset Limited
Website: https://apel.com.ng
Search online: apel asset nigeria

APT Securities and Funds Limited
Website: https://www.aptsecurities.com/index.php
Search online: apt securities nigeria

Capital Assets Limited
Website: https://capitalassets.com.ng
Search online: capital assets nigeria

Cardinalstone Securities Limited
Website: https://cardinalstonesecurities.com
Search online: cardinalstone securities nigeria

Chapel Hill Denham Securities Limited
Website: https://www.chapelhilldenham.com/securities-trading
Search online: chapel hill denham securities nigeria

Cordros Securities Limited
Website: http://securities.cordros.com
Search online: cordros securities nigeria

Coronation Securities Limited
Website: https://www.coronationsl.com
Search online: coronation securities nigeria

CSL Stockbrokers Limited
Website: https://www.cslstockbrokers.com
Search online: csl stockbrokers nigeria

EFG Hermes Nig. Limited
Website: https://www.efghermes.com
Search online: efg hermes nigeria

FBNQuest Securities Limited
Website: https://fbnquest.com
Search online: fbnquest securities nigeria

Greenwich Trust Limited
Website: https://www.gtlgroup.com
Search online: greenwich trust nigeria

Meristem Stockbrokers Limited
Website: https://www.meristemng.com
Search online: meristem stockbrokers nigeria

Morgan Capital Securities Limited
Website: http://www.morgancapitalgroup.com
Search online: morgan capital securities nigeria

Qualinvest Capital Limited
Website: https://qualinvestcapital.com
Search online: qualinvest capital nigeria

RenCap Securities (Nigeria) Limited
Website: http://www.rencap.com
Search online: rencap securities nigeria

Stanbic Ibtc Stockbrokers Limited
Website: http://www.stanbicibtcstockbrokers.com
Search online: stanbic ibtc stockbrokers nigeria

Tellimer Capital Limited
Website: https://tellimer.com
Search online: tellimer nigeria
Note: At present, this brokerage firm only deals with institutional investors or corporate clients, not individuals.

United Capital Securities Limited
Website: https://www.unitedcapitalplcgroup.com/securities
Search online: united capital securities nigeria

Nigerian International Securities Limited
Website: https://www.nisl-ng.com
Search online: nigerian international securities

Readings Investments Limited
Website: https://readingsinvestmentsltd.com
Search online: readings investments nigeria

Selected mutual funds:

ARM Aggressive Growth Fund
Fund managers: ARM Investment Managers
Website: https://arminvestmentmanagers.com/portfolio/arm-aggressive-growth-fund
Search Online: arm nigeria aggressive growth fund

AXA Mansard Equity Income Fund
Fund managers: AXA Mansard Investments Limited
Website: https://www.axamansard.com/investments/equity-income-fund
Search Online: axa mansard nigeria equity income fund

FBN Nigeria Smart Beta Equity Fund
Fund managers: FBNQuest Asset Management
Website: https://fbnquest.com/asset-management/products/
mutual-funds
Search Online: fbn nigeria smart beta fund

Legacy Equity Fund
Fund managers: FCMB Asset Management
Website: https://www.fcamltd.com/index.php/
investment-management/fcam-mutual-funds-2/
legacy-equity-fund-2
Search online: csl nigeria legacy equity fund

Meristem Equity Market Fund
Fund managers: Meristem Wealth Management Limited
Website: https://meristemwealth.com
Search online: meristem equity market fund

Stanbic IBTC Nigerian Equity Fund
Fund managers: Stanbic IBTC Asset Management Limited
Website: https://www.stanbicibtcassetmanagement.com/
nigeriaassetmanagers
Search online: stanbic ibtc nigerian equity fund

INDEX

A

AGM xxi, 38, 86, 117, 121, 129, 131, 132, 133, 152

Annual general meeting xxi, 38, 131, 132

Annual report 121, 131, 132

B

Bank Verification Number xxi, 39

Bearish stock 89, 90, 91, 93

Bear market 6, 7, 8, 92, 95

Bid price 65

Bids 19, 58, 65, 74, 75, 125

Bonus share 5, 98, 116, 117, 118

Bullish stock 94

Bull market 6, 7, 8, 93, 95

BVN Scheme 39

C

Capital appreciation 2, 3, 53, 54, 55, 66, 93, 94, 95, 115, 123, 126

Capital gain 2, 5, 18, 23, 55, 82, 107, 125, 128, 130, 139, 150

Capital gain reinvestment 139

Central Securities Clearing System xiii, xxi

CHN xxi, 43, 51, 97, 99, 111

Clearing House Number xxi, 43

Compound interest 140

Corporate action 5, 64, 69, 70, 126, 133, 152

CSCS xiii, xxi, 19, 20, 36, 41, 43, 44, 45, 51, 80, 81, 97, 98, 99, 100, 117, 118, 128, 136, 152

CSCS online account xiii, 36, 45, 97, 99, 118, 152

W

Withholding tax 23, 79, 82

X

X-Alert 36, 97, 100, 101

Printed in the United States
By Bookmasters